WOMEN AND MINISTRY
IN THE NEW TESTAMENT

Elizabeth M. Tetlow

Paulist Press
New York/Ramsey

Library of Congress
Catalog Card Number: 79-57398

ISBN: 0-8091-2249-9

Published by Paulist Press
Editorial Office: 1865 Broadway, New York, N.Y. 10023
Business Office: 545 Island Road, Ramsey, N.J. 07446

Printed and bound in the
United States of America

CONTENTS

For my daughters

Tania
Maria
Sonia
Sarah

PREFACE

There are serious questions being raised in the Church today concerning the role of women in ministry. The Second Vatican Council asserted that "since in our times women have an ever more active share in the whole life of society, it is very important that they participate more widely also in the various fields of the Church's apostolate."[1] This position was reaffirmed by the third Synod of Bishops, meeting in Rome in 1971. "We also urge that women should have their own share of responsibility and participation in the community life of society and likewise of the Church."[2]

Yet women are in fact and by law excluded from the official ordained ministry of the Church.[3] What are the reasons, present and historical, why this is the practice of the Church? The Sacred Congregation for the Doctrine of the Faith attempted to answer this question in 1976. It justified the exclusion of women from ordained ministry on the basis of the constant tradition of the Church, which, it said, was rooted in the practice of Jesus and of the apostles. It summarized the present position of the magisterium in the statement that "the Church, in fidelity to the example of the Lord, does not consider herself authorized to admit women to priestly ordination."[4]

The crux of the problem is located in the understanding and interpretation of the practice of Jesus and the apostles. The available information on this subject is contained within the New Testament. The tradition of the Church has always accorded a primary place of authority to the word of scripture. In recent times Vatican II reiterated the belief that scripture contains and presents "divinely revealed realities" which "have been committed to writing under the inspiration of the Holy Spirit." Therefore "the books of Scripture must be acknowledged as teaching firmly, faithfully, and without error that

1

truth which God wanted put into the sacred writings for the sake of our salvation."[5] Thus according to the teaching of Vatican II whatever scripture says about a subject has a normative value for the Church. If a conflict arises between the practice of the Church and the word of scripture, the Church should conform its practice to the revealed word of God.

If the situation were actually so simple, all problems could be resolved by following the letter of the text of scripture. But this is not the case. One complicating factor is the fact that scripture presents the word of God in translation. God did not dictate the New Testament in Greek. The word is presented through the language of the evangelist or epistolographer. This language is conditioned by the history, culture and theology of the historical writer. Thus it is impossible for the reader today to establish exactly what word of God is being revealed in a given text of scripture without the mediation of interpretation. What is important is that the element of interpretation be consciously recognized and be in accord with the most rigorous scholarly standards.[6]

Biblical scholarship is a science which is constantly learning and growing. Thus it is possible that an understanding of a text which was generally held ten years ago may today be viewed as incorrect. Many of the past interpretations of biblical texts on the subject of the ministry of women were filtered through the theological presupposition that Jesus could not possibly have called women to ministry nor could the early Church have possibly permitted women to function in ministry since women are essentially inferior to men and their divinely established role in life is one of subordination to men in all things.

In the present moment in history there is a newfound freedom from the presuppositions of the past. For the first time, scholars are able to look at the question of the ministry of women in the New Testament without being bound by the traditions of women's inferiority and subordination. Because of this freedom, scholars are beginning to discover information about the role and ministry of women in the primitive Church that had never before been noticed.

This book will seek to reevaluate the question of the ministry of women in the New Testament. In its interpretation of the biblical texts it will employ the results of current biblical scholarship and attempt to remain free of the culturally conditioned presuppositions of other eras.

The journey will not be either short or simple. The ministry of women in the New Testament is a broad and complex question. It cannot be comprehended adequately without some knowledge of its context: the social and religious position of women in the Mediterranean world in the first century A.D. Thus a preliminary question must first be explored. What did it mean to be a woman in the time of Jesus? What were the status and roles of women in Hellenistic Greek society, in Roman society, and in intertestamental Judaism?

There is a second and equally important preliminary subject to be discussed before proceeding to the major question. What is the meaning of ministry? What is the nature of Christian ministry according to the New Testament? What was its background in the history of religious office in Old Testament Judaism? What was the nature of Jesus' own ministry? What did Jesus teach his followers about the kind of ministry to which he was calling them? What were the earliest forms of ministry in the primitive Church? What were their antecedent models? Were these ministries authentically conformed to the nature of ministry lived and called for by Jesus?

After these two preliminary issues have been clarified, there remains the central task of the book: to examine the New Testament evidence concerning the ministry of women in the time of Jesus and in the first century Church. Did Jesus himself call women to ministry? Were women included in or excluded from apostolic ministry according to the New Testament? Were the ministries exercised by women in the early Church official ministries of the Church? Is there anything inherent in the character of Christian ministry as presented by the New Testament which would give reason for the inclusion or exclusion of women?

The author would like to express her gratitude to those colleagues and friends who helped make this a better book than it would have been without their encouragement, insights and criticisms. First of all, I would like to thank Donald L. Gelpi, S.J. of the Jesuit School of Theology at Berkeley for the initial inspiration to begin reflecting on the subject of ministry, for the invitation to contribute two chapters on the biblical foundations of ministry to his own book on the theology of ministry, and for his helpful criticism of the manuscript at each stage of its development. I would also like to thank Kathleen M. Gaffney of Xavier University and Gerald M. Fagin, S.J. and John R. Stacer, S.J. of Loyola University in New Orleans for generously giving of their time to read and criticize the manuscript in its entirety. Any errors or omissions in this work must, of course, remain the sole responsibility of the author. The greatest debt of gratitude is owed to my husband, Mulry, for giving me the freedom of time and space necessary to research and write this book, and for his generosity in taking time from his own busy schedule of teaching and counseling to type the manuscript.

New Orleans
Pentecost, 1979

NOTES

1. *Apostolicam Actuositatem,* 9. Walter M. Abbott, (ed.), *The Documents of Vatican II* (New York: America Press, 1966), p. 500.
2. "Justice in the World" (Washington: United States Catholic Conference, 1972), p. 44.
3. *Codex iuris canonici* 968, 1.
4. "Declaration on the Question of the Admission of Women to the Ministerial Priesthood" (Rome, October 15, 1976), no. 5 (cf. no. 6). Text in Leonard Swidler and Arlene Swidler (eds.), *Women Priests. A Catholic Commentary on the Vatican Declaration* (New York: Paulist, 1977), p. 38.
5. *Dei Verbum,* 11. Abbott, *op. cit.,* pp. 118–119.
6. Cf. Pius XII, *Divino afflante Spiritu* (1943); *Dei Verbum* 12, 23.

CHAPTER ONE:
THE STATUS OF WOMEN
IN GREEK, ROMAN AND
JEWISH SOCIETY

Introduction

The social world of the Mediterranean in the time of Jesus had a long and complex history. Israel was not the only great civilization in ancient times. In the East there had been Akkadians, Hittites, Assyrians and Persians among others, and in Palestine itself there had been Canaanite city-states. These societies had been for the most part patriarchal, relegating women to an inferior and subordinate position.

Most societies in the ancient world were patriarchal. There were, however, a few exceptions. In the third millennium B.C. the Sumerians accorded women a position which was almost equal to that of men. Women were, for example, able to own and control the use of property. They were educated and legally able to take more than one husband. In the second millennium, however, Sumerian men achieved supremacy and reduced the rights and status of women from that time on.[1]

In the West, Egypt was another exception. The status of Egyptian women was high and their legal rights approached equality with men throughout the last three millennia B.C.[2] Marriages were monogamous and commonly by mutual consent. Women had equal rights in inheritance.[3] Because of these rights many women were able to become wealthy and through their wealth acquire political power. A few women even ruled as pharaohs.[4]

The civilization of Sumer died out and its place in the East was taken by patriarchal societies. The civilization of Egypt on the other hand survived. By the time of the hellenistic period, the continuous tradition of freedom, education and equality of women in Egyptian society was beginning to have an influence on the position of women in Greek society in other parts of the hellenic empire. The Romans also encountered the influence of Egypt as Julius Caesar and later Mark Antony mingled their destinies with its queen, Cleopatra VII.

By the first century the eastern part of the empire was firmly committed to patriarchy and the subordination of women. In the West, at least in Egypt, women were educated, free and almost equal in status to men. Greek and Roman societies were between the two extremes. In both there was a tension of opposites: a patriarchal ideal of the silent and obedient wife, working in seclusion within the home, and the reality of historical women who owned wealth and property and exercised a role in political society. The real women of history were constantly challenging the patriarchal ideal of male dominance and superiority.

Judaism in the first century had emerged from the oriental patriarchal tradition in which women were considered the property of men with no rights, no role in society except childbearing, and no education. In the intertestamental period Judaism was, however, affected by its encounter with hellenism. This produced a double effect. Some schools within Judaism reacted negatively, attempting to reinforce the subordination and seclusion of women in order to safeguard the purity of Judaism against the influence of hellenism. In the diaspora this was often impossible. The Jewish people were living within hellenistic society. There were Jewish women who had acquired wealth and education within that society.[5] Such women were beginning to have a voice in business and politics. Many Jews lived their everyday lives more according to the mores of hellenistic society than those of Torah and Talmud. Greek philosophical and theological ideas began to be taken up by Jewish philosophers and theologians.[6]

It was into this complex world that Christianity was born. Christianity originated in the Judaism of Palestine, which was itself partially hellenized. It soon spread to Greece, Egypt and Rome. It was within the experience of its encounter with these cultures that the Christian faith was formulated and its scripture composed. In these lands of the first-century Mediterranean world, the earliest Church made decisions about the position and role of women within the Christian community. Such decisions were inevitably affected by the context of Jewish, Hellenistic or Roman culture in which they were made. This chapter will examine the question of the status and religious role of women in Greek, Roman and Jewish societies in the centuries that preceded the birth of Christ.

WOMEN IN ANCIENT GREECE

The quest for historical information about the status of women in ancient Greek society is a lively issue among scholars today.[7] There are a variety of available sources into which the historian may delve for information about women: ancient historians, biographers, orators, philosophers, poets and playwrights, as well as data found in the fine arts, in inscriptions and papyri, and in urban and religious archaeology.

Scholars have long debated whether the earliest social and religious structures were matriarchal. Matriarchy has many shades of meaning, from a society in which the roles of men and women are equal to one in which women rule and men are subordinate. At least among the heavenly hierarchy of ancient Greece goddesses at first predominated. Hesiod's *Theogony*, which was composed around 700 B.C., described the shift in power from the earlier goddesses, whom he associated with passions and evil forces, to the rational heroic male god, Zeus. Once he had gained power, Zeus established a patriarchal order among the gods. Thenceforth male gods were free to exploit goddesses and earthly women at their pleasure.

The Late Bronze Age

In the eighth century B.C. the blind poet Homer described the period of the Trojan War which had taken place near the end of the Bronze Age, four centuries earlier.[8] Many powerful and influential women appeared in the Homeric epics, among them the Greek queens Helen, Clytemnestra and Penelope. Marriage was frequently matrilineal, that is, the inheritance passed from mother to daughter. The right of Helen to leave her husband and enter into a new mar-

riage with Paris was not challenged. The probable reason why Menelaus and his allies went to war over the issue was that Menelaus' own
right to the throne of Sparta lay in his status as Helen's husband. If
she married another, he would lose his right to political and economic power in the city-state. Likewise after Agamemnon had departed,
Clytemnestra herself held the rule of Mycenae. She proceeded to
take a new husband and together they continued to rule, finally kill-
ing Agamemnon upon his return. During Odysseus' absence, Penelope was besieged by suitors, probably not so much because she was
personally attractive, but rather because she ruled the wealthy and
politically important city-state of Ithaca.

    In general, Homer portrayed these ancient women within the
framework of his own patriarchal values. Sons were valued more
than daughters. Wifely fidelity was praised, while the double standard was taken for granted. Men could be polygamous and most had
slave concubines. Women generally stayed indoors and performed
domestic tasks. Upper-class women had slaves to do the more menial
jobs. It is quite possible, though, that this portrait of women reflected
not only Homer's own experience in the eighth century, but the actual practice in the twelfth century. Mycenian tablets reported that the
food allotment for men at the time was two and a half times that of
women.[9] Such would tend to indicate that the position of women was
inferior to that of men.

Archaic Greece (800–500 B.C.)

    The records of the archaic period are very sparse. The law codes
of two city-states do give some information on the status of women
there in the latter half of the period. The law code of Sparta was
composed in the seventh century and was attributed to Lycurgus.
The most important role of women in archaic Sparta was the bearing
of children. For this reason women were to be fed equal rations, educated and trained in athletics. Women were able to marry at a later
age than in other city-states and therefore faced less danger of death
in pregnancy and childbirth. Toward the end of the period many
women in Sparta had become quite wealthy and reduced the popula-
tion by refusing to bear many children.[10] Spartan women were portrayed by Plutarch as heroic and proud.[11]

    The law code of Gortyna on Crete dates from about the same

time.[12] There women had the right to own, control and inherit property. A certain percentage of what a woman produced through her work belonged to her. In divorce a woman retained half her property.

It is known that there were at least nine women poets during this period. A few are known by name, such as Corinna and Sappho, but little of their poetry has been preserved. These women were educated and belonged to the upper class of society. Thus they enjoyed the freedom and the leisure to be able to write. None of them lived in Athens.[13]

Athens in the Classical Period (500–323 B.C.)

The situation of women in archaic and classical Athens was far more restricted than in other Greek city-states. Women were generally excluded from education and political life. The sixth-century law code of Solon legalized prostitution, reflecting social acceptance of the double standard.

There has been some debate among scholars whether women were totally secluded in Athens or whether they enjoyed some measure of freedom.[14] The truth probably lies in between the two extremes. There is evidence that there were very definite expectations for the different sex roles. These did, however, vary somewhat among different socio-economic classes.[15] Women were not completely secluded in ancient Athens, although many men would have liked to see them so. Women did, to some extent, seek a role and a voice in their society. Yet they did not enjoy full social or political freedom as such.

The primary duty of women in ancient Athens was to marry and to bear legitimate children so that their family unit might continue. If there was no son, a daughter might inherit, but was obligated to marry her next of kin. A dowry was given at marriage for the support of the wife. It was to remain intact during the marriage while she received eighteen percent interest on it annually.[16] Divorce might be initiated by either partner, but there are few records of divorces initiated by the wife, who had to be aided in the procedure by her father. In divorce, the children were considered the property of the husband and remained with him.

Marriages were arranged by parents. A girl was expected to

marry by the time she was fourteen. This left few years for her education, which was confined to the home and concerned primarily with domestic affairs. Women were expected to work, but within the home. They spun and wove and managed their slaves. The homes had separate women's quarters.[17] When their husbands entertained guests, women were not permitted to be present. Yet women did go out of the home to attend festivals and funerals. It is probable, but not certain, that they were able to go to the theater.

Attic literature of the period generally portrayed women as inferior and of dull and unpleasant character.[18] It was thought that women should not be educated since that would make them more dangerous to men.[19] One of the least misogynistic writers in classical Greek literature was Euripides. He portrayed many of his women characters as strong and noble self-sacrificing heroines. Such women were frequently depicted as stronger and nobler than their male counterparts.[20] He also pictured women as victims of patriarchal exploitation.

The greatest proximity to a concept of equality for women in the classical period is in the utopian literature. In the ideal society there would be no private property and therefore no need for legitimate heirs. Women were allowed far greater freedom and the right to participate in politics. Plato described his view of the ideal society in the *Republic*.[21] There women were to be educated for the good of the state. Competent women would be able to become guardians and in that position they would rule over both men and women. Women were also to be trained to fight to defend the state. In the *Laws* Plato presented another, less idealistic sort of utopia. There he retreated to limiting women to the traditional sex roles of classical Athens, although he did still affirm education of women.[22] In general women were expected to obey men. Even in the *Republic* Plato noted that the place of woman was within the confines of her home.[23]

Aristotle had an even lower view of women than his teacher. He believed that inequality between men and women was based upon the law of nature. Man is superior, woman inferior. Husbands and fathers should rule over their wives and daughters.[24] Only men were thought capable of philosophy and the virtues. The role of women was obedience and silence. It has been suggested[25] that the writings of Aristotle codified the general social practice and mores of Athens during the classical period.

In 430 B.C. Pericles proclaimed that "the best reputation a woman can have is not to be spoken of among men for good or evil."[26] Women were kept in the shadow in classical Athens. Yet they were permitted to testify in court, were generally literate and had some understanding of economics and politics.[27] The seclusion and silence of women was the cultural ideal. It is not certain that all women were willing to comply with such an ideal in actual historical fact.

Plutarch: A Later View of Classical Greece

In the first century A.D., Plutarch wrote his *Moralia* explaining the customs and mores of the ancient Greeks. His works reflect the same ambivalence found in Plato. He described the ideal woman, employing the example of an heroic woman who had helped to liberate her city-state. Even such a woman, after her heroic deed, then withdrew into seclusion in the women's quarters, never again meddling in politics, and spending the rest of her days quietly weaving among her family.[28]

In marriage, even if the wife contributed the larger part of the estate, it was more fitting that the entire estate be said to belong to the husband.[29] Wives were to be seen only in the company of their husbands. Otherwise, they were to remain secluded and silent.[30]

On the other hand Plutarch did express his disagreement with Thucydides that women should always be silent.[31] He admitted that women should be educated in philosophy, literature, geometry and astronomy.[32] The husband might serve as the teacher of his wife. Then husband and wife could share in the fruits of education by having a more stimulating life together.[33] In case of disagreement, husbands ought to persuade their wives through the use of reason, not force.[34] Plutarch also thought that they should eat meals together.

Plutarch made reference to women prophets and poets.[35] He noted the general literacy of married women and praised women who possessed political wisdom.[36] He gave examples of women who exercised a political role. One such woman in Phrygia administered the government of her city-state and did so "excellently."[37]

The women portrayed in Plutarch's *Moralia* come from all areas of Greece. This may account for the greater freedom and education of women than was common in classical Athens. It is also possible that Plutarch reflected some of the mores of Roman and Hellenistic society in his own times.

Summary

Women in classical Greece did have some education and some role in society. Both were likely to be greater if they did not live in Athens. However, neither their education nor their social role was equal to that of men of the same socio-economic class. Women did not have the freedom to determine their own lives. There was a saying in ancient Greece, at various times attributed to Thales, Socrates and Plato, in which man thanked the gods that he was not uncivilized, a slave, or a woman.[38]

Hellenism

The hellenistic period extended from the time of Alexander the Great in the late fourth century until the Roman conquests in the first century B.C. Culturally Hellenism continued to exercise an important influence in the Roman empire in the first centuries A.D.

Alexander the Great brought the era of the Greek city-states to an end. They were replaced by a vast cosmopolitan empire. This fact had a great impact on all aspects of social life and culture. As society changed, so the position and role of women within society also changed.

The hellenistic queens in Greece, Syria and Egypt held real political power. The mother of Alexander, the Macedonian queen Olympias, ruled Greece when her son was away on his conquests. In Egypt, Arsinoë II co-ruled with her husband, Ptolemy II. The images of both appeared on contemporary coins. Cleopatra VII ruled in her own right at the end of the hellenistic period.[39]

Yet the situation of women at this time was far from ideal. Their marriages were arranged. Even the marriages of queens were political alliances. In hellenistic Egypt, brother-sister marriages were common in ruling families, in order to preserve economic power within the family unit. Kings practiced polygamy. The wife who was most adept at political intrigue and even murder was the one who survived and gained power in the hellenistic courts.

Women in the colonies lacked the forms of male protection which they had known in Greece. Consequently they had to learn to protect themselves. Marriage and family life were weakened as the empire expanded. One of the most effective resources of women in this period was economic power. Through their personal wealth women were able to gain legal rights and a voice in public affairs. Many women were honored for their generosity toward the state. In the first century B.C. a woman magistrate was honored for building a reservoir and an aqueduct.[40] Both the accomplishments and the political office of the woman may have been a function of her own personal wealth. In Sparta at this time women owned forty percent of the land and exercised great political and economic power.[41]

Laws varied in different regions of the empire. In Egypt women had the right to make contracts and wills and the obligation of taxation. Distinctions were made between Greek and Egyptian women. The former required a male guardian in order to make a legal contract; the latter did not. In Greece women had the right to conduct business, make loans and manumit slaves with the approval of their guardians.[42]

Hellenistic marriage contracts stated rights and obligations for both spouses, although these were different for husband and wife. In the case of divorce the dowry was returned to the wife and the husband had to continue to support the children. The communal property, however, was retained by the husband.[43] The double standard prevailed and was recognized. Husbands could take concubines and prostitution was legal.

Upper-class women received some degree of education and many were literate. In hellenistic Egypt there was greater literacy among women than among men.[44] There were hellenistic women poets, such as Erinna, some of whose verses are extant.[45] In 218 B.C. Aristodama, a woman poet of Smyrna, was granted honorary citizenship by the Aetolians.[46]

The dominant philosophical schools of the Stoics and Neopythagoreans excluded women and emphasized traditional sex roles.[47]

They were challenged by the Epicureans and the Cynics. The Epicureans admitted women on an equal level to their school. There was a woman philosopher among the Cynics named Hipparchia who taught in public with her husband.[48]

When the parochial Greek city-states became a worldwide empire great changes occurred in society and mores. Women exercised political power with skill. Political and economic power made some women equal in status to men. Other women became competent professionals in athletics, music, poetry, literature, philosophy, oratory, medicine and various crafts.[49] Class barriers were breaking down and the institution of the family was weakened. Traditional social roles of the sexes were challenged and this resulted in controversy and conflict.[50] A man could no longer presume his wife's compliance with a role of seclusion, passivity and silence. The challenge had come, not from a change in philosophic or social ideals, but from the concrete fact of historical women who possessed real economic power and who used it to struggle for freedom and equality.

The Religious Role of Women in Ancient and Hellenistic Greece

Frescoes of the ancient Minoan civilization on Crete portray many women priestesses. They wore special ornate dress and danced in the sacred olive grove as part of the religious cult. Goddesses were pictured surrounded by female dancers. Male priests were fewer in number and dressed in the same style of clothes as the women priests.[51]

From the time of the installation of Zeus at the pinnacle of the hierarchy of the gods, the role of women in traditional Greek religion became subordinate to that of men. Even the rites of the goddesses were dominated by male priests.[52] Some cults excluded women from any form of participation.[53]

There was a woman "priest" of Apollo at Delphi who was called a Pythia. She was usually a middle-aged, celibate, uneducated woman who was chosen and then trained by the male priest. Her role was to go into a trance, possibly under the influence of drugs, during which she would utter gibberish. This was then interpreted by the male priests according to their own political research and an oracle was given by them to the petitioner.

The woman priest of Athena Polias, the patron goddess of Athens, was important and influential in the political life of the city in the classical and hellenistic periods. The office was hereditary in a prominent noble family. On the annual feast of the Panathenaea, women and men participated in the processions and young virgins carried baskets.[54]

Plutarch made reference to women priests of Dionysius who were involved in a political demonstration, using their office to influence the political authority at Elis.[55] He also mentioned a woman priest of Demeter who performed marriage ceremonies.[56]

The role of women in traditional Greek religion was generally more restricted than it was in the syncretistic mystery cults which came to prominence in the empire during the hellenistic period. Many women converted to the mystery religions. It is possible that some of these conversions were motivated by the greater role women were permitted to play in the mystery cults. Some of the cults disregarded social and sexual roles completely. The cult of Agdistis in Philadelphia admitted men and women, free persons and slaves. The Eleusian mysteries from the fourth century B.C. on admitted women, slaves and Greek-speaking foreigners.[57]

In the Eleusian mysteries the highest office was held by a male chief priest. The lower ranking priests were both men and women. The woman priest of Demeter and the male chief priest were each paid a small coin by every initiate. Events at Eleusis were dated according to the name and year in office of this priestess. Some women priests were married, others lived in celibate communities.[58]

Women were able to exercise a leadership role in the mystery religions.[59] Women priests and religious functionaries were publicly honored in hellenistic society.[60] The mystery religions did not, however, proclaim the social equality of women. In general they held a negative view of sex and demanded continence before and during their rites. Asexual spiritual marriage was practiced. Although such a view to some extent freed women from being regarded and treated merely as sex objects, it ultimately reinforced the theory of their inferiority. If sexual relations were considered evil, it was because contact with women was believed contaminating, not contact with men.

WOMEN IN THE ROMAN EMPIRE
The status of women in the Roman empire was influenced by the position of women in hellenistic society and also in the earlier Italian civilization of Etruria. The Etruscans had accorded women great freedom and respect. Women were allowed to participate independently in society and business.[61]

In the Roman empire many women possessed great wealth. Influenced by the example of hellenistic queens who had also lived in an empire where their husbands were frequently absent on campaigns for long periods of time, Roman women began to exercise political power. Yet they rarely actually held political office. They sometimes ruled in the name of their absent husband or son who held the title of the office. In other parts of the empire women fared better in attaining political office, although it is possible that their titles were merely honorific.[62] Women also influenced the men who held office through their economic power.

In theory, traditional sex roles were still accepted by Roman society. This fact created tension between the theoretical ideal of the woman staying at home and weaving, and the reality of historical women moving with relative freedom in the political arena and marketplace.

According to Roman law women were under the complete control of the *pater familias,* the male head of the extended family unit. This power extended to life and death. A death penalty could be imposed upon a woman for adultery or drinking alcohol.[63] The *pater familias* arranged marriages and appointed guardians for the women of his family. A woman could not legally transact business, make a contract or a will, or manumit a slave without the approval of her guardian.[64] However, a woman might request a new guardian or a reversal of a decision by a guardian by submitting her case to a magistrate. By the time of Augustus a free woman was exempt from the control of a guardian after she had borne three children; a freed woman after the birth of four.[65] The law of guardians was not rigidly enforced and women frequently did transact business independently of them.

There were different types of marriage in Roman society. In *manus* marriage the woman left the control of the *pater familias* and came under the jurisdiction of her husband. This type of marriage tended to be more stable. In non-*manus* marriage the woman remained under the authority of her *pater familias,* which tended to give her more freedom.[66] Some women actually chose their own spouses.[67] Most women married between the ages of twelve and fifteen. Widowhood and divorce were common. Divorce could be initiated by either spouse or by the wife's father. Few divorces at the request of the wife are recorded. The husband retained custody of the children. In subsequent marriages at a later age, women had greater choice in the selection of a spouse.

Cornelia, the mother of the Gracchi, was an influential Roman woman who was honored because, as a widow with twelve children, she refused an offer of marriage from a hellenistic prince in fidelity to the memory of her late husband.[68] Well educated, Cornelia wrote letters which were later published. She had great political influence during the reigns of her sons. She continued to entertain learned guests in her home after her sons had been assassinated.[69] Widows with few children were, however, exhorted to remarry. Widows who committed suicide upon the death of their husbands were greatly honored.[70]

The double standard was upheld by law. Only the adultery of a woman was a crime which required punishment. Prostitution was legal. Marriages and divorces were arranged on the basis of political and economic reasons. Daughters were not given individual names. They were called by the feminine form of the name of their father. If there were more than one daughter, they were numbered.[71] Infanticide, especially of girl babies, was practiced.

Yet Roman women had a legal right to inherit. They amassed great fortunes. The role of a wife was to manage the household. All chores were done by slaves, although the ideal wife was still expected to spin and weave like her ancient ancestors. The women of the upper classes were in reality free from work. They were able to go out: to market, to festivals, to attend banquets in mixed company. Status in Roman society was sought through public display of wealth. Some women in the imperial court were actually proclaimed gods in the state cult of emperor worship.[72] Shrines were erected to them in the provinces and their images were found on coins. Statues and buildings were erected in Rome to honor important men and women. Women were able to petition the Senate and even held protest demonstrations against oppressive laws.[73]

Women were expected to supervise the education of their children. The education of women was valued in Roman society. It was possible for girls to attend school. Women studied music, philosophy, literature, grammar and geometry. In the first century A.D. the Roman Stoic Musonius Rufus urged that women receive the same education as men.[74] Roman women wrote letters, memoirs and poetry. They presided over literary salons.[75] There were women painters and women physicians.[76]

Among the lower classes in Roman society women received a smaller allotment of grain than did men and boys. Freedwomen sold merchandise in the markets, formed trade guilds, lent money, did laundry and served as waitresses. Men and women slaves could take paying jobs and save their money to buy their freedom.[77] In some ways lower-class Roman women enjoyed greater freedom than women of the aristocracy. There were fewer restrictions on morality and marriage and less supervision.[78]

Thus women in Roman society did exercise a public role. They held real political and economic power. Yet they were restricted for the most part from holding political offices. Women were always legally and theoretically subordinate to men. Women of the upper classes were able to become well educated. This increased the possibility of their being respected by men. The status of women in Roman society was never in fact, however, equal to that of men.

The Role of Women in Roman Religion

The Romans had an official state cult of Vesta, goddess of the hearth, of domesticity and continuity of family and state. The head of this cult was the *pontifex maximus.* Under him there was a college of pontiffs. There is no feminine form of the word *pontifex.* Women were excluded from the highest office in Roman religion.

Under the authority of the pontiffs were the vestal virgins, who had the task of tending the sacred hearth-fire of the state. The Romans considered this function so important that the welfare of the state was thought to depend upon it. A virgin who let the fire go out was publicly flogged. One who was involved in sexual immorality, which was thought to pollute the cult, was buried alive.[79]

The vestal virgins were all daughters of patrician families until the time of Augustus.[80] There were six altogether. The eldest had au-

thority over the others. When a position fell open, twenty candidates
were selected from among whom one virgin was chosen by lot. The
service began between the ages of six and ten and lasted for thirty
years. After having completed thirty years of service a virgin was free
to retire and to marry. But most were by that time rather old to find
a suitable marriage partner and preferred to continue in office where
they enjoyed power and authority that increased with age and senior-
ity.

The vestal virgins were the only Roman women who were legally independent of the authority of the *pater familias.* When they entered the service they were given a share of property over which they
retained ownership. They played an official role in some festivals.
Their position was highly visible as they rode through the streets in
special chariots and were given the best seats at banquets, spectacles
and the theater. Important political documents and wills were entrusted to their care. They sometimes even influenced emperors.[81]
The vestals were, however, always under the authority of the pontiffs.

The wives of priests were sometimes priestesses. The *flaminica*
was the wife of the *flamen dialis* and a priestess of Juno. When she
died her husband's priesthood was terminated.[82] In the cults of the
imperial family in the provinces, there were women priests serving
the divinized empresses.[83]

Some cults, such as those of Hercules and Mithra, admitted
only men. Others, such as the cult of the *Bona Dea,* admitted only
women. A woman magistrate presided over this cult and the vestal
virgins also played a role in it. Some of the women's cults admitted
only those of a certain social or marital class. The cults of Patrician
Chastity and Womanly Fortune admitted only patrician women of
no more than one husband (*univiri*). The cult of Plebian Chastity admitted plebian *univiri.* The cult of Virile Fortune was especially for
prostitutes. These cults of Fortune and Chastity tended to reinforce
traditional sex roles and mores for women.[84]

The Romans imported Greek priestesses for the hellenistic mystery cult of Ceres and granted them Roman citizenship.[85] This was a
women's cult comprised of matrons and virgins. It excluded men and
persons of the lower classes. The Egyptian mystery cult of Isis was
also popular in the Roman empire. In Roman inscriptions naming

twenty-six priests (*sacerdotes*) of Isis in Italy, six of these priests were women. They were women of both the upper and lower classes.[86] Frescoes in Pompeii and Herculaneum depict women participating in the rites of Isis. This cult was considered revolutionary by the Roman authorities and it was suppressed several times.

Thus in the Roman empire women did exercise an official role in religion, although they were not admitted to the highest religious offices. Religion was ultimately controlled by men. Even cults admitting only women were frequently used by the male authorities to reinforce the subordinate role of women. Roman men and women were permitted to convert to new religions as long as these were not seen as threatening to the well-being of the state.

WOMEN IN JUDAISM

Women in the Old Testament

The opening chapters of the Old Testament present two very different stories about creation and attitudes toward woman. The older yahwistic account in Genesis 2 describes the creation of man, Adam, from the dust of the earth. Woman is created only later and out of the body of the man. The narrative continues in Chapter 3 with the story of the fall. Later tradition interpreted these passages to mean that woman from the first moment of her existence was by nature subordinate to man and the source of all sin and evil.

This creation story does not fully represent the thought of Israel on the subject either of creation or of woman. Several centuries later another account of creation was composed by priestly editors. Such was its importance in their eyes that it was set as an introduction to the entire Pentateuch. In this story in Genesis 1, man and woman are created at the same time. Both are fashioned in the image of their creator (1:27). Both are blessed and commissioned by God to fill the earth and rule over it (1:28). It is significant that woman as well as man was said to image God and to receive God's blessing and commission.

In general women in the Old Testament were legally the property of men.[87] This condition is characteristic of patriarchal societies. Before marriage the girl was the property of her father. After marriage a woman became the property of her husband.[88] Widows were placed under the authority of their fathers, sons or brothers-in-law.[89] Polygamy was common. Women were considered objects of property among the spoils of war.[90]

The ten commandments are an example of early, yet continuous, legal tradition of Israel. Stylistically they are addressed to men. The last commandment lists a wife among objects of property which are not to be coveted. Yet men are also exhorted to honor mothers as well as fathers, and to allow both women and men to rest on the sabbath.

A woman achieved some measure of social status by becoming the mother of a son. Conversely, a sterile woman was divorced. Sarah and Rebecca were especially revered as the mothers of Israel. The narratives about the patriarchal period, although written much later, mention some freedom of women to appear in public.[91] Later Hebrew women generally led a harem-like existence, confined within the home. As time went on, the restrictions gradually became more elaborate and were combined with formal penalties for their transgression. The patriarch ruled family and clan in Hebrew society. Inheritance passed from father to son. Men could initiate divorce at will. Women were bound in marital fidelity.

Somehow a few Hebrew women did manage to exercise a leadership role in public life. In the period of the settlement, Deborah led the people Israel as judge and as military commander in battle against the Canaanites. Queen Athaliah ruled the southern kingdom for six years after the death of her son, Ahaziah.[92] A late hellenistic book presents a literary portrait of another Hebrew queen, Esther, in legendary Persia.

A number of women are named in the Old Testament as functioning in the important religious office of prophet: Miriam, Deborah, Huldah, the wife of Isaiah, and Noadiah.[93] Hymns whose composition was attributed to women stand among the oldest religious literature of Israel.[94] There is also mention in the Old Testament of women sages.[95] Women were, however, totally excluded from the religious office of priest in Israel.

According to the Torah, women were impure during times of menstruation and childbirth. They were impure twice as long after the birth of a daughter as after the birth of a son. Any contact with women at such times rendered a man ritually unclean. Women also were thought to contaminate any object they touched. Ritual purity was of primary importance in the Jewish tradition of priesthood and temple cult. A major reason why women were excluded from the priesthood and from full participation in the temple cult was their frequent ritual impurity. Even within the synagogue women were kept at a distance and seated in an area segregated from the men.

Post-Biblical Judaism

In the intertestamental and early rabbinic periods Judaism stood in constant struggle to preserve its identity against the influences of secular hellenistic culture. As a result, in many areas it reacted against the social advances which were taking place in the empire. Judaism frequently adopted the strictest, most literal interpretations of the Torah, and encased these within elaborate rubrics and further regulations.

In the apocrypha and pseudepigrapha of the intertestamental period women were generally portrayed as temptresses and evil sex objects. Men were strongly advised to avoid all possible contact with women except what was necessary for the procreation of children. Foreign women were thought to be especially dangerous. One book went so far as to state that women as such were evil.[96]

Rabbinic literature expressed an even more stridently misogynistic attitude toward women. Women were described not only as evil temptresses, but also as witches and nymphomaniacs.[97] They were further caricatured as greedy, vain, lazy and frivolous.[98] Rabbinic society was for the most part monagamous, but polygamy was still permitted to men. Divorce was compulsory if a wife was childless for ten years. Male children were viewed as preferable to female children. Every morning each Jewish man prayed in thanksgiving to God that he had been created a man and not a woman.[99]

Wives were generally to be confined to the home. In the presence of others their heads had to be covered and faces veiled. When male guests were invited women were not allowed to eat meals with their families. All conversation between men and women was discouraged.[100] Women were not permitted to receive any education. Legally they were still considered the property of men. Their testimony was not accepted as evidence in court.

In Jewish religion women were also kept subordinate and silent. Women were more restricted in Judaism than they had been in the Old Testament.[101] They could not recite the prayers at meals. They were not obligated as men were to go up to Jerusalem to participate in the major pilgrim festivals. Women were barred from studying the Torah.[102] They could not be counted among the *minyan,* the quorum of men who had to be present for worship to take place. Theoretically any adult person had the right to read and to preach in the synagogue.[103] But in practice women were kept physically separate from men in the synagogue and were not allowed to read at all. Furthermore, women were denied the education which would have enabled them to preach.

Sectarian Judaism

There were different opinions concerning the position of women among the various Jewish sects. The Essene literature of Qumran is quite negative both toward women and sex. It was a celibate community which was dominated by priests. There was no real place for women either theologically or in the reality of its existence in the desert wilderness of Judaea.

In the diaspora, on the other hand, Jewish sects were more greatly affected by the experience of hellenism and foreign cultures. In the Jewish colony at Elephantine in Upper Egypt women could own property and transact business, take oaths and initiate divorce. They were also taxed and called up for military service.[104] The Therapeutae, an Essene-like sect living in Egypt, were also much more positive in their attitude toward women than the Essenes of Palestine. The Therapeutae admitted women to full membership in the community. Women were, however, still segregated and silent during worship. Both the Elephantine colony and the Therapeutae may have been influenced by the freedom and high position of women in Egyptian society.

Philo and Josephus

Philo was a hellenistic Jewish philosopher living in first century Alexandria. He resisted the influence of his Egyptian environment and viewed women as inferior and evil creatures.[105] Their proper place was in seclusion and in subordination to men, ruled by father or husband.[106] He believed that man was led by reason and woman by sensuality.[107] Influenced by the spirit-matter dichotomy of neo-platonism, he viewed sex, which involved contact with matter, as evil.[108] Spiritual man, according to Philo, did well to avoid contact with sensual woman. On the other hand, he did advocate some, but not equal, education for women.

The Palestinian Jewish historian Josephus spent part of his later life in Rome. As a Jew he accepted the theoretical inferiority of women. As an historian living within the Roman empire he described a number of influential women in his historical works.[109] He made note of the quite normal resentment of Alexandra, the mother of Mariamne, at Herod's restriction of her freedom. On the other hand he reiterated that women could not be witnesses and were segregated during worship.[110] It is the Jewish view of woman that emerges as dominant in the thought of Josephus:

> The woman, says the Law, is in all things inferior to the man. Let her accordingly be submissive, not for her humiliation, but that she may be directed; for the authority has been given by God to the man.[111]

Conclusion

The position of women in the Mediterranean world of the first century differed from culture to culture. In general it is possible to say that women were nowhere totally free or equal. Yet Hellenistic, Roman and Egyptian women did enjoy some degree of freedom and exercised a real political, economic, and religious role in their societies. First century Judaism lived in the Roman empire and in the cultural milieu of Hellenism. It was unable to ignore secular culture, but had to react to it positively or negatively.

Christianity was born into this complex and syncretistic world. The societies of this world still by and large advocated the traditional role of subordination and silence of women as the ideal. Yet in real life the women of history were neither subordinate nor silent. The ideal was challenged in the forum of real life. The tension and conflict generated by this challenge were the social milieu in which New Testament Christianity was formulated.

NOTES

1. Samuel Noah Kramer, "The Goddesses and the Theologians: Reflections on Women's Rights in Ancient Sumer," unpublished address to the *Rencontre Assyriologique Internationale* XII (Rome, July, 1974). Cited by Leonard Swidler, *Women in Judaism* (Metuchen, New Jersey: Scarecrow, 1976), pp. 4–5.

2. From 2778 B.C. until 30 B.C., with the exception of a few brief periods of feudalism. Cf. Swidler, *Women in Judaism,* pp. 5–6.

3. Swidler, *Women in Judaism,* pp. 5–7.

4. Queen Hatshepsut (eighteenth dynasty) reigned from 1503 to 1482 B.C.

5. Ac 13:50. Lydia, in Ac 16:14–15, was a "Godfearer."

6. Philo, Wisdom.

7. Cf. Marylin B. Arthur, "Classics," *Signs* 2(1976), pp. 382–403 for a review of the literature and the state of the debate.

8. 1184 B.C. is the traditional date of the fall of Troy.

9. Sarah B. Pomeroy, *Goddesses, Whores, Wives, and Slaves* (New York: Schocken, 1975), p. 30.

10. Plutarch, "Life of Lycurgus," 14–16. Cited in Mary Lefkowitz and Maureen B. Fant, *Women in Greece and Rome* (Toronto: Samuel-Stevens, 1977), pp. 52–54. Cf. Pomeroy, *op. cit.,* p. 38.

11. Cf. Plutarch, *Lacaenarum Apophthegmata* II, 240c ff. Cited by A. Oepke, *"Gyne,"* in Gerhard Kittel, *Theological Dictionary of the New Testament* (Grand Rapids: Eerdmans, 1964–74), I, 777. Henceforth this work will be abbreviated *TDNT.*

12. 7th/6th century B.C. It is preserved in a 5th century inscription.

13. Pomeroy, *op. cit.,* p. 56.

14. Cf. Arthur, *art. cit.,* p. 389, and H. D. F. Kitto, *The Greeks* (Baltimore: Penguin, 1951), pp. 219–220. The strongest position on the freedom of Greek women was taken by Arthur W. Gomme, "The Position of Women in Athens in the Fifth and Fourth Centuries B.C.," *Essays in Greek History and Literature* (Oxford: Blackwell, 1937), pp. 89–115, although few scholars have agreed with him.

15. Pomeroy, *op. cit.,* p. 60.

16. *Ibid.,* p. 63.

17. Aristophanes, *Thes.* 414 ff., 790 ff., noted that women were kept in the women's quarters where they were guarded by dogs. Cf. Oepke, *TDNT* I, 777.

18. Oepke, *TDNT* I, 777, cites examples from Sophocles and Menander.

19. Menander, Fr. 702. Cited by Oepke, *TDNT* I, 777.

20. For example, Alcestis and Polyxena in Euripides, and also Antigone, Ismene and Deianira in Sophocles.

21. Plato, *Republic* V, 453e–457e.

22. Plato, *Laws* VII, 802e, 814, VIII, 833d, 834d.

23. Plato, *Republic* IX, 579b.

24. Aristotle, *Politics* I, 12.

25. Arthur, *art. cit.,* p. 394.

26. Pericles, "Funeral Oration," trans. in Kitto, *op. cit.,* p. 221.

27. Arthur, *art. cit.,* p. 393.

28. Plutarch, "Bravery of Women," *Moralia* III, 257e.

29. Plutarch, "Advice to Bride and Groom," *Moralia* II, 140ff.

30. *Ibid.,* 139c, 142d.

31. Plutarch, "Bravery," 242e.

32. Plutarch, "Advice," 138c.

33. *Ibid.,* 146a.

34. *Ibid.,* 139e.

35. Plutarch, "Bravery," 243a.

36. *Ibid.,* 252a, 255e.

37. *Ibid.,* 263c. Cf. 257e.

38. Diogenes Laertius, *Lives of Eminent Philosophers* I, 33. Cf. Oepke, *TDNT* I, 777, n. 4.

39. According to Plutarch, "Life of Mark Antony," 25–27, Cleopatra VII spoke at least nine languages. Cited in Lefkowitz-Fant, *op. cit.,* p. 127.

40. Cf. Pomeroy, *op. cit.,* pp. 125–126.

41. Pomeroy, *op. cit.,* p. 38.

42. *Ibid.,* pp. 127, 130.

43. *Ibid.,* pp. 128–129.

44. Swidler, *Women in Judaism,* pp. 18, 179, n. 68.

45. Pomeroy, *op. cit.,* p. 137.

46. *Ibid.,* p. 126.

47. For example, in the Pythagorean community in Italy in the 3rd/2nd century B.C., men were to be politicians and philosophers, while women were to keep house and care for their husbands. Courage and intellect were considered male qualities, chastity the quality of a woman. Cf. Lefkowitz-Fant, *op. cit.,* p. 85 for texts.

48. Cf. Abraham Malherbe (ed.), *The Cynic Epistles* (Missoula, Montana: Scholars Press, 1977), pp. 54–55, 78–83, 94–95, 172–175, 282–285.

49. Swidler, *Women in Judaism,* pp. 14–15. Lefkowitz-Fant, *op. cit.,* cites inscription about Polygnota of Thebes, a woman harpist, p. 13, and Diogenes Laertius on the woman philosopher Hipparchia, p. 12. Cf. n. 48 above.

50. Wayne A. Meeks, "The Image of Androgyne: Some Uses of a Symbol in Earliest Christianity," *History of Religions* 13(1974), p. 206.

51. S. Alexiou, *Minoan Civilization* (Heraklion: Alexiou, 1969), pp. 41, 44, 105–106.

52. Mary Rose D'Angelo, "Women and the Early Church: Reflecting

on the Problématique of Christ and Culture," L. and A. Swidler, *Women Priests*, pp. 196, 201, n. 38.

53. For example, the cults of Delphi, Hercules and Aphrodite Acraia on Cyprus. Cf. Swidler, *Women in Judaism*, p. 21; Oepke, *TDNT* I, 786.

54. Pomeroy, *op. cit.*, p. 75.

55. Plutarch, "Bravery," 251e.

56. Plutarch, "Advice," 138b. In the fourth century B.C. Demosthenes referred to a woman, Phano, who, as wife of the archon, performed sacrifices for the state (*Contra Naera*, cited in Lefkowitz-Fant, *op. cit.*, p. 37). There is also mention of a woman priest of Demeter and Kore in the 2nd/3rd century A.D. (inscription cited in Lefkowitz-Fant, *op. cit.*, p. 194).

57. Meeks, *art. cit.*, p. 169.

58. Pomeroy, *op. cit.*, pp. 76–77.

59. Swidler, *Women in Judaism*, p. 21. The role of women in the Isis cult is debated. Cf. D'Angelo, *art. cit.*, p. 201, n. 38.

60. Pomeroy, *op. cit.*, p. 125.

61. Swidler, *Women in Judaism*, p. 22, cites evidence of paintings, epitaphs and tombs.

62. According to some inscriptions, wealthy Greek women held offices and Roman citizenship in the provinces, although the offices may have been honorific. Cf. Arthur, *art. cit.*, p. 401. Swidler, *Women in Judaism*, p. 24, notes that in Pompeii there were inscriptions of names of women candidates for office. Dio Cassius, *History of Rome*, 78–79 (cited in Lefkowitz-Fant, *op. cit.*, p. 122) mentioned that the mother of Caracalla had been appointed "to receive petitions and to have charge of his correspondence in both languages." However, according to Livy, *History of Rome* 34, 1–8, (cited in Lefkowitz-Fant, *op. cit.*, p. 138) Roman women could not hold "magistracies, priesthoods, triumphs, badges of office, gifts or spoils of war."

63. A. Gellius, *Attic Nights X*, 23, citing Cato. Cited in Lefkowitz-Fant, *op. cit.*, p. 147.

64. Table V of the Twelve Tables. Cited in Lefkowitz-Fant, *op. cit.*, p. 134.

65. Pomeroy, *op. cit.*, p. 151.

66. *Ibid.*, p. 155.

67. *Ibid.*, p. 157.

68. Ptolemy Physcon.

69. Pomeroy, *op. cit.*, p. 150.

70. *Ibid.*, p. 161.

71. For example, Julia I, Julia II, and so on. Cf. M. I. Finley, *Aspects of Antiquity* (New York: Penguin, 1977), pp. 125–126, Pomeroy, *op. cit.*, p. 150.

72. For example, the wife and daughter of Julius Caesar.

73. Pomeroy, *op. cit.*, p. 177. Women demonstrated against the Oppian Law in 195 B.C.

74. Musonius Rufus, *In stob. ecl.* II, 235, 24ff. Cited by Oepke, *TDNT* I, 780.

75. References in Pomeroy, *op. cit.,* pp. 172–173, 177.

76. Pliny, *Natural History* 35, 40, mentions women painters. Inscriptions of the first and second centuries A.D. mention women physicians. Cited in Lefkowitz-Fant, *op. cit.,* p. 172.

77. Pomeroy, *op. cit.,* pp. 200, 203. Inscriptions mention women seamstresses, dressmakers, hairdressers, stenographers, scribes, secretaries, silk-slaves, fishmongers, and wool-weighers. Cited in Lefkowitz-Fant, *op. cit.,* p. 182.

78. Finley, *op. cit.,* p. 131.

79. A vestal virgin was thus executed in A.D. 83, during the reign of Domitian. Cf. Plutarch, "Life of Numa," 9–10.

80. In A.D. 5 Augustus allowed freed women to apply.

81. J. P. V. D. Balsdon, *Roman Women* (London: Bodley Head, 1962), p. 238.

82. *Ibid.,* pp. 242–243.

83. *Ibid.,* p. 243. Cf. inscriptions in Lefkowitz-Fant, *op. cit.,* pp. 152, 193, which mention women priests in the imperial cults in Aphrodisias and Pompeii.

84. Arthur, *art. cit.,* p. 402; Pomeroy, *op. cit.,* pp. 206–208.

85. Pomeroy, *op. cit.,* p. 216. There were also women priests of these cults in the provinces. Cf. inscription of 1st century A.D. which mentions a woman high priest of Asia, in Lefkowitz-Fant, *op. cit.,* pp. 192–193.

86. Pomeroy, *op. cit.,* p. 226.

87. Gn 3:16. Cf. Oepke, *TDNT* I, 781.

88. 1 Sm 18:17.

89. Men could refuse to enter into levirate marriage; women could not. Dt 25:5–10. Cf. Oepke, *TDNT* I, 781.

90. Nm 31:18, Dt 21:10–14.

91. Gn 24:15–21, 29:6–12, 34:1 Also texts from the period of the settlement: Jdg 21:21, Ruth 2:2–3.

92. 2 Kg 11.

93. Ex 15:20, Jdg 4:4, 2 Kg 22:14–20, Is 8:3, Neh 6:14.

94. Ex 15:21 (song of Miriam), Jdg 5 (song of Deborah).

95. 2 Sm 14:2–20, 20:15–22, Jdg 5:29.

96. Test Reub 5:1–2. Cf. Jub, Test XII Pat.

97. Hillel, Aboth 2, 7, bKeth 65a. Cf. Swidler, *Women in Judaism,* p. 198, n. 78.

98. Gen rabb 45, bQid 49b, 82b. Cf. Oepke, *TDNT* I, p. 781.

99. R. Yeh.ben Elaj, TBer 7, 18, jBer 13b, bMen 43b. Cf. Oepke, *TDNT* I, p. 777.

100. Oepke, *TDNT* I, pp. 786–787.

101. bErub 53b, Ab 1, 5. Cited by Oepke, *TDNT* I, p. 781.

102. jSota 10a8: "May the words of the Torah be burned, they should

not be handed over to women." Cf. Sota 3, 4, bSota 216. Cited in Oepke, *TDNT* I, pp. 781–782.

103. Meg 23a.

104. Cf. Swidler, *Women in Judaism,* pp. 69–70.

105. Philo, *Hypothetica* 11, 14–17.

106. Philo, *Flaccus* 89, *De spec. leg.* III, 169–171.

107. Philo, *De opif. mund.* 165, *Leg.all.* 38–39.

108. Philo, *De spec. leg.* III, 113.

109. Josephus, *Antiquities* VII 11, 8, XI 3, 5, *War* I 5, 1 (Queen Alexandra), VII 9, 2 (Masada).

110. Josephus, *Antiquities* V 8, 15.

111. Josephus, *Contra Apion* II, 201. Trans. by H. St. J. Thackeray, *Loeb Classical Library* (Cambridge: Harvard University Press, 1966), p. 373.

CHAPTER TWO:
THE BIBLICAL FOUNDATIONS
OF CHRISTIAN MINISTRY

RELIGIOUS OFFICE IN THE OLD TESTAMENT

The religious milieu in which Jesus lived his own ministry and in which the early Church began to select the forms of its ministry was predominantly that of late Judaism in Palestine. Judaism in the intertestamental period, although influenced from the outside to some extent by hellenism and other currents of oriental syncretism, was primarily grounded from the inside on the rock of Old Testament scripture. To understand the character of Jesus' own ministry and to comprehend the meaning of the forms of ministry chosen by the earliest Christian community, it is necessary to have some knowledge of the forms of religious office portrayed in the Old Testament.

From the time of the exile, and even earlier, it is possible to distinguish two traditions of ministry and worship in the Old Testament. First there is the tradition of cult, sacrifice and temple. The ministry for this type of worship was restricted to the levitical priesthood. But there was also a second tradition of worship and office which was centered in the word. The forerunners of this tradition were the prophets and sages of ancient times. After the exile the ministers of the word were wisdom teachers, scribes and rabbis. This became the Torah-centered tradition of the synagogue.

In the time of Jesus both traditions were important in the religious life of Palestinian Judaism. Both were available models upon which Jesus and the early Christian community might draw in defining the character of Christian ministry and religious office within the nascent Church. Some knowledge of the meaning of each of these traditions in the Old Testament is an essential prerequisite for understanding the development of Christian ministry in the New Testament.

The Tradition of Priesthood

The dominant tradition of worship and religious office in Israel before the exile was that of the priesthood and temple cult. But priesthood and cult did not appear out of a vacuum. They have a history, and this history had an influence on the character of the office as it later developed.

The History of Priesthood in Israel

During the early period of the Israelite monarchy, the people began to seek understanding about how the important offices of king and priest came into being. Stories were composed about an earlier time, an age of great patriarchal ancestors. The patriarch was the head of his family and clan. As such he was also the religious leader of the clan and their representative before God. The patriarch built altars and shrines, consecrated them and offered sacrifices to God. The office of patriarch has been called a form of "natural priesthood" since the patriarch exercised priestly functions based upon his position within the family and clan rather than upon official consecration. There are numerous stories in the book of Genesis about the cultic activities of the major patriarchs, Abraham, Isaac and Jacob.[1] Each was portrayed consecrating sanctuaries and offering sacrifices to God.

Levi is named among the twelve sons of Jacob and the twelve tribes of Israel.[2] It is not certain whether the tribe of Levi was actually considered priestly from the beginning, or whether it was originally a secular tribe which later became specialized in cultic office.[3] Exodus twice mentions the existence of priests in Israel before the formal institution of the tribe of Levi as priests by Moses at Sinai.[4] There was, however, no well-defined order of priesthood until the ratification of the Sinai covenant.

Moses himself is called a priest only in Psalm 99:6, but never in the Pentateuch. The Yahwist account of Moses' birth in Egypt affirms his levitical ancestry.[5] The priestly editors of the Sinai narrative, however, recognized only Moses' brother Aaron and Aaron's

sons as legitimate priests. Moses was portrayed as anointing Aaron
and his sons as priests with oil and with blood from the sacrifice.[6]

Moses was the last individual whom the priestly tradition in the
Old Testament described as approaching God directly. After the establishment of the covenant, priesthood and cult at Sinai, thenceforth it was the function of the priest to mediate the relationship
between the people and God. The social and religious importance of
the priests increased in proportion to the exclusiveness of their claim
to the right to this function.

During the period of the settlement in the promised land, members of the tribe of Levi began to take over the cultic functions of the
people. For the first time in this period there are historical texts
which were actually composed during the time that they describe.
The situation which is presented is that there were at first many Levites in the south. The tribe of Levi was becoming increasingly specialized in cultic activity. There were too few cultic positions in the
south, so many Levites migrated north seeking employment. Gradually they put non-levitical ministers both in the south and later in the
north out of business. The levitical priests achieved economic securi-
ty by asserting their exclusive rights to exercise cultic functions
through clan solidarity against all competitors.[7]

The title "priest" *(kōhēn)* and the concept of priestly office seem
to have been of Canaanite origin.[8] This type of office emerged in
most ancient near eastern cultures as they reached a certain degree of
sedentary urban civilization.[9] In Israel the institution of priesthood
developed around established sanctuaries, many of which had originally been Canaanite. Priestly families arose to prominence at the
major shrines of Dan, Nob and Shiloh.[10]

During the monarchy the history of the priesthood became increasingly complex. At the beginning of the monarchy the levitical
house of Eli moved from Shiloh to Nob where they were massacred
by Saul. Only Abiathar escaped. When David became king, he made
Abiathar, who was the sole heir of the priesthood of the most powerful sanctuary in Israel, and another unknown and mysterious figure,
Zadok, the official priests of his new royal capital, Jerusalem. When
Abiathar supported Adonijah, Solomon deposed him and made Zadok the sole official priest of his reign.[11] From that time until the sec-

ond century B.C. the house of Zadok controlled the official priesthood of the Jerusalem Temple.

Who was this Zakok? One scholarly theory is that Zadok was
the Jebusite[12] priest of Jerusalem before David conquered the city.[13]
David then simply allowed him to continue in that position after he
took over, possibly to make his own authority more acceptable to the
Jebusite inhabitants of the city. If this were true, it would have been
necessary to legitimize the priesthood of Zadok in the eyes of Israel.
This may have been the intention of two Old Testament passages
which date from this period: Genesis 14 and Psalm 110. Both refer to
the archetypal ancestor of the Jebusite priesthood at Jerusalem, Melchizedek, and to the recognition of Melchizedek's priesthood by
Abraham, the archetypal ancestor of Israel. Both would lead the
reader to conclude that if Abraham recognized the priesthood of
Melchizedek, then the contemporary Israelite could accept the legitimacy of the priesthood of Zadok.[14]

The reform of Josiah in 621 B.C. was a turning point in the history of Israelite priesthood. Before that time shrines still existed outside of Jerusalem and each shrine had its own priesthood. The Josian
reform put a definitive end to the provincial shrines and centralized
all worship in the Jerusalem Temple. Sacrifice henceforth was permitted only in the Temple and could only legitimately be offered by
the temple priesthood.

Many Israelites lived outside of Jerusalem and were unable to
travel to the city to worship very frequently. The centralization of
the priestly cult in Jerusalem created a situation in which other
forms of worship began to develop which were independent of priesthood and cult.

In the Temple itself a hierarchical structure of clerical offices
was developing. Some of the provincial levites who migrated to Jerusalem after the closing of the shrines found work in the Temple as
menial functionaries. At the summit of the hierarchy there was one
official priest who was head of the house of Zadok and chief of the
temple clergy.[15] When Nebuchadnezzar conquered Jerusalem in 587
B.C. there were a chief priest and a "second priest" who administered the Temple, and three "keepers of the threshold" who were in
charge of collections.[16] Under them were the "elders of the priests"

who were the heads of the various priestly families. At the bottom of the hierarchy, under the ordinary priests, were the singers and gate-keepers, some of whom were levites. Women had no place in the hierarchy. They were permitted only the task of serving outside the entrance to the Temple.[17]

In 587 B.C. the highest priestly classes were deported into exile in Babylon. The Temple of Jerusalem was destroyed and the traditional cult ceased. The cultic role of the king came to a permanent end. The catastrophe of the exile made persons of different classes into peers. This led to power struggle and polarization. The former ruling classes sought restoration of their power based upon models of their own institutions. The formerly oppressed classes sought power based upon archaic models and a program of revolution.[18]

The powerful and aristocratic zadokite temple clergy had been taken into exile in Babylon. The poor client levites had been left in the land. It is possible that those who remained in Palestine during the exile performed cultic functions at the site of the ruined Temple.[19] Whatever form their ministry had taken, these priests and levites had enjoyed complete freedom of ministry for more than half a century. The conflict was inevitable when their former zadokite superiors returned from Babylon.

The restoration program of the zadokite aristocracy is recorded in the book of Ezekiel. The pre-exilic zadokite temple structures were transformed into a program for a future ideal hierocratic state. Only zadokites were to function as priests in the new temple.[20] An explicit distinction was made between priests and levites. Only priests were considered sufficiently holy to approach the presence of God. Levites were to function only as temple servants.

Before the exile there is no recorded zadokite claim to aaronic descent. During the restoration the zadokite clan sought to increase and legitimize their authority by establishing roots in the traditions of Torah and Yahwism through a new genealogy linking their ancestry to Aaron. Those priests who could not prove their descent from Aaron were excluded from priestly service in the Second Temple.

In the year 445 B.C. Ezra promulgated the final priestly edition of the Pentateuch, which was thenceforth recognized as sacred scripture and as law. The actual powers of the priests were thereby transformed into legal institutions.[21] In the "priestly code" all priests were declared "sons of Aaron." Aaron himself was presented as the first high priest. The ritual actions, vestments and regulations of purity of the Second Temple were ascribed to institution by Moses himself. Priests and levites were represented as distinct from the very beginning. Levites were shown not to be descended from Aaron. They were described as being given to the priests to be their servants.[22]

The zadokite control of the temple priesthood came to an end in 172 B.C. with the deposition of Jason. The Hasmonean rulers later appointed themselves to the office of high priest. But many Jews rejected them as illegitimate because they were not members of the zadokite clan.[23]

During the Roman period the high priesthood became a political appointment with no regard for genealogical legitimacy.[24] The office ceased to be held for life. The frequent replacement of high priests created a new class of high priestly families in Jerusalem. These formed an influential aristocracy at the time of Jesus. The high priesthood itself, however, was no longer the supreme authority it had been in the Persian period.

When the Roman legions destroyed the Second Temple in 70 A.D. the active functioning of the priesthood and the cult itself came to a final end. Priestly ministry and cultic worship thenceforth ceased to exist in Judaism. They were replaced by the ministry of the word.

The Nature of Israelite Priesthood

The priesthood of Israel was an exclusive and élite professional caste in which there was membership only on the basis of birth. A man was born a priest if he could trace his ancestry through Aaron to Levi. Priesthood was a caste which specialized in the performance of the cult. In the last five centuries of its existence, the primary function of Israelite priesthood was to officiate at the rites of animal sacrifice in the Jerusalem Temple.

After the exile and the demise of the monarchy, the high priest replaced the king as the most important and influential political figure in the nation. Since all worship had been centralized by law in the Temple, the temple priesthood had complete control over the cult. They were paid taxes and stipends for their services and thereby became quite wealthy in many periods of history. Priesthood in Israel was an institution of power, which was both political and economic.

The priest was understood as the representative of God to the people and of the people to God. Thus he stood in the middle, between the two, as mediator. Other religious offices, such as that of prophet, were governed by divine charism. For the priesthood, technique replaced charism. The priest was the person who knew the proper rites and rituals to influence God to be favorable to the petitioner's request. The performance of such rites was generally bought and sold for money or goods.

The institution of priesthood reflected a theology of God as transcendent, holy and set apart from his people.[25] The priest, as mediator between this unapproachably transcendent deity and the people, himself took on some of the qualities of the deity he represented. Priests came to be viewed as themselves holy and set apart from the people. There was an acute awareness of ritual impurity or lack of holiness as a barrier to entering the presence of the holy. Only the priests had access to God's presence. This was ultimately restricted only to the high priest and that only once a year on Yom Kippur. Women, who were generally viewed as ritually impure, were totally excluded both from the priesthood and from access to the presence of God. Priesthood was the most completely male dominated religious institution in Israel. It was the only religious office from which women were excluded by law. There was simply no question that a woman could ever serve as priest in Judaism.

Installation into the Office of Priest

Ordination, understood as incorporation into a new order, did not take place in Israelite priesthood. Priesthood was understood as an office, not a vocation. A person was born a priest by virtue of his ancestry. God had chosen the archetypal ancestors, Levi and Aaron. It was not necessary that he choose the descendent.

Priests were installed into the service of a particular sanctuary. In the early history of Israel there were various forms of installation ritual. One early form was the ceremony of the "filling of the hands,"[26] in which a symbol of the stipend he would receive in the service of the sanctuary was placed in the hands of the new priest. Later a new priest was given parts of the sacrificial victim, symbolizing his share in the revenues of the sanctuary. Another rite of installation was the imposition of hands. It was performed by the people.[27] It symbolized the offering of the first-born to God, for which the priest acted as substitute. This rite was not used only for priests. Joshua was installed in the secular office of leader of the people through the imposition of hands by Moses.[28] After the exile the high priest was installed into office in a tripartite ceremony of purification, investiture and anointing.[29] The ritual of anointing was extended to other priests in later times.[30]

A man was born a priest, then installed into the priesthood of the Temple or a sanctuary. Through service in the sanctuary he came to be viewed as further set apart from the people. Thus through his work the priest took on a greater aura of holiness. It was imperative that he observe all the special regulations of ritual purity in order to enter the holy place. These regulations and ritual practices then served to set him even further apart from other people and attached an even greater sense of holiness to his person.

Thus in Israel a man became a priest by birth and was consecrated and set apart through his functioning as a priest. A ceremony of installation was not necessary to make him a priest, only to install him officially into a particular priestly position. Ultimately it was the grounding of priesthood upon genealogy that made any sort of ordination unnecessary.

The Meaning of Priesthood in Israel

Admission to the priesthood in Israel was determined by genealogy. Call by God, possession of his gifts, merit or competence were totally irrelevant. Priests were viewed as holy, but this was understood in terms of observance of regulations and rites, not in terms of goodness or sanctity.

The object of priestly ministry was not the people or their spiritual needs, but the cult itself, its practice and preservation. In its social consequences, priesthood in Israel came to mean power, élite status and membership in an exclusive caste which held itself above and apart from the rest of the people. Like any human institution it was subject to internal corruption, which was frequently proportionate to the amount of power it held at the time. The history of the office was one of almost continual conflict, feud and power struggle.

Priesthood in Israel was primarily a conservative force, dedicated to preserving its own power and status, its cult and itself as an institution.

The Tradition of the Word

Priesthood and sacrifical cult were not the only forms of ministry and worship in Israel. From the very beginning of the monarchy there is written evidence of the activity of prophets and wisdom teachers. Although prophecy and wisdom were themselves independent schools, the two traditions are alike in emphasizing the word and standing apart from the cult. They are also similar in the practice of grounding religious office upon call and competence, not upon clan membership or genealogy.

The Prophetic Tradition

The prophet was a person who was called by God to speak his word. The person, man or woman, was called on the basis of God's choice, not on the basis of personal status or ancestry. When God chose an individual as his prophet, he then gave that individual the gifts necessary to carry out the call. Thus prophecy in Israel may be described as a charismatic office. The prophet was called and gifted to proclaim God's word of covenant and promise, of judgment and redemption.

Prophecy emerged in Israel as part of a revival of Yahwism against the threat of Canaanite syncretism centered in the priestly cult of the provincial shrines and sanctuaries. Again and again the prophets called the people and their priests away from idolatry of cult and back to the word of Yahweh. Often the people did not want to listen to the harsh words of the prophets. Sometimes their refusal to listen and return to the word is portrayed by the Old Testament writers as resulting in national disaster. God called prophets and commissioned them to proclaim his word. When the people did not listen and repent, foreign armies destroyed the nation and even its Temple.

Only a few of the prophets committed their prophecy to writing. The writing prophets lived during a period of less than three centuries.[31] The most active years of prophecy in Israel were before the exile. Many prophets were associated with the monarchy. One of the functions of the Israelite prophet was to challenge the king. Some prophets lived at the royal court. With the demise of the monarchy after the exile, the office of prophet also came to an end. Post-exilic writers began to speculate about the coming of a future prophet in the messianic age.

The primary difference between prophecy and priesthood was that the prophet communicated with God on the basis of personal relationship and charism. The priest consulted God through the use of sacred objects and cultic techniques, and on the basis of membership in a special caste.[32] The priesthood was itself a power structure, whereas the prophets generally challenged existing power structures.

Another difference between priesthood and prophecy was a contrasting view of the role of women. Women were totally excluded by law from the office of priesthood. But women were called to the office of prophet which they exercised on the same basis as men. Five women prophets are named in the Old Testament: Miriam, Deborah, Huldah, the wife of Isaiah, and Noadiah.[33] The prophet Joel envisioned both men and women prophesying in the future ideal age.[34]

The Wisdom Tradition

The wisdom tradition was a continual factor in the history of Israel from earliest times. King Solomon modeled his court on the courts of Egypt, collecting wisdom teachers around himself as court officials. In later centuries wisdom schools grew and spread throughout the land.

In the earliest wisdom literature of Israel there is mention of wise women: the wise women of Tekoa, of Abel and of the court of Sisera.[35] Later the wisdom schools were dominated by men. Women were excluded not only from teaching wisdom, but also from studying it. Ironically the post-exilic wisdom schools personified both Wisdom and Torah as feminine figures with many stereotypical feminine roles and attributes. Both Wisdom and Torah were exalted almost to a state of divinity as feminine hypostases of God active in the world.

Whereas the priest and the prophet were more concerned with the religious life of the people as a whole, the wisdom teacher addressed the individual person and educated him in the traditions of wisdom. Priesthood and prophecy were theocentric. Priesthood pre-

sented a transcendent God who was far distant from the people and
unapproachable in holiness. Prophecy presented a God who was
transcendent, but who was also very concerned about and involved
in the moral and religious conduct of his people. Wisdom on the other hand was more anthropocentric. It focused on the human person
in the midst of ordinary life on this earth. This included the person's
relationship to God. The wisdom teacher taught how to live in
wholeness and dignity in relationship with fellow human persons and
with God. A man became a wisdom teacher on the basis of study and
competence which were recognized by the community that he
served.

　　　After the exile, when kingship and prophecy had ceased, it was
the wisdom tradition which responded most effectively to the crisis
and gave it theological meaning. After the return to Palestine the
temple cult was restored but no longer met the religious needs of all
the people. Other non-cultic forms of worship had been discovered
during the exile in Babylon when there was no temple cult available.
The law and the word of scripture had become the axis of Jewish religion. Scribes such as Ezra emerged from the wisdom schools, teaching and interpreting the Torah. Other places of worship called
synagogues were established in Babylon and later throughout Palestine. Wisdom schools came to be located in the synagogues, and the
wisdom teachers who taught there later came to be called scribes and
rabbis.

The Synagogue Tradition

　　　According to rabbinic tradition the Torah was handed down directly by Moses through the prophets to the hundred and twenty elders of the "Great Synagogue" as Israel returned to Palestine after
the exile. These men were said to have instituted the prayers of synagogue worship.[36] The tradition of the Great Synagogue and its elders
as the religious leaders of Israel after the exile was based upon rabbinic exegesis of Nehemiah 8–10. Historically it is not known for
certain when the synagogue originated. Rabbinic tradition, Philo and
Josephus traced it all the way back to Moses. This view was, however, based upon legend. The prototype of the synagogue began to develop in the seventh century B.C. when worship was centralized in

Jerusalem and the provincial shrines closed down and their clergy exiled. During the Babylonian exile the development of non-sacrificial worship became an urgent need since during the decades of exile it was the only form of worship available to the Jewish people. After the return the synagogue tradition continued to grow both in the diaspora and in Palestine where it existed for centuries side by side with the temple cult. It became not merely a substitute for temple worship, but an important form and tradition of worship in its own right. By the first century A.D. there were synagogues in every town and village in Palestine, and even one within the precincts of the Temple itself.[37]

In late Judaism the synagogue tradition gradually increased in importance as the temple tradition diminished in importance. In the Greek and Roman periods, scribes and rabbis came together in the Pharisee party and dominated the religious life of the synagogue. After the destruction of the Second Temple in 70 A.D. the rabbis came to dominate the entire religious thought, literature and worship of Judaism.

In the time of Jesus the synagogue formed the religious tradition and worship of Galilee, as it did in all the regions of Palestine outside of Jerusalem. The Temple was still important and people went up to Jerusalem on the great pilgrim festivals. However, four decades after the death of Jesus the Temple was destroyed by Roman legions. In the diaspora Jewish communities were already totally independent of the temple tradition and united in the synagogue. Thus at a time when the early Church was still in its period of formation in the areas of ministry and worship, the tradition of the word superseded the tradition of priesthood and cult as the sole form of ministry and worship in Judaism. This fact was one among many influences on the development of early Christianity.

Religious Offices in the Synagogue

The office of wisdom teacher, scribe and rabbi was a teaching office, proclaiming and interpreting the word of God to the people. It was based upon individual competence and acceptance by the community. There was another office in the synagogue tradition which was an office of administration, of judging and sometimes also of proclamation of the word. This was the office of elder, an ancient institution which emerged out of the patriarchal structures of Israel's pre-history.

The office of elder in Israel, as in other ancient near eastern societies,[38] was based upon the authority of age and the wisdom which presumably accompanied it. The Hebrew word for elder, zāqēn, literally meant "one who wore a beard." The earliest historical texts in the Old Testament mention the existence of the office of elder. During the period of the settlement, elders were chiefs of clans and heads of families.[39] Somewhat later they formed the collective governing bodies of the towns.[40] They played a role in the establishment of the monarchy and in its politics, including those of the divided monarchy. It was the elders, not the priests, who anointed David king.[41] Elders continued to play an important political role during the exile[42] and in the Persian[43] and Greek periods.[44]

Elders performed judicial, as well as administrative functions. They sat at the town gates and judged disputes.[45] Later they formed judicial institutions.[46] When someone was killed by an unknown murderer, the elders of the nearest town were supposed to kill a heifer to prevent a blood feud.[47]

Elders also performed religious functions. They are portrayed in the Old Testament as representing the people before God at important moments in the history of Israel: at the exodus and the ratification of the covenant at Sinai.[48] In the Sinai narrative in Exodus 14, the elders were allowed to approach the presence of God as closely as Aaron, who symbolically represented the priesthood of Israel. In Exodus 18:12 it was Aaron and the elders who shared in eating the bread of Jethro's sacrifice. In Numbers 11:16–26 the Elohist writer presented Moses choosing seventy elders from among the elders of Israel and communicating to them the divine Spirit which rested on him.[49]

The elders of Israel were the forerunners of the elders of the synagogue. The latter were selected by co-optation and then chose from among their number the "head" of the synagogue.[50] Synagogue elders were installed in office by prayer and the imposition of hands.[51] Elders were given seats of honor in the synagogue and permitted to interpret the Torah. Some of their interpretations were preserved and collected.[52]

The highest offices in the synagogue were voluntary lay offices. The elders ruled the synagogue. The head of the synagogue was the chief administrator. Under the elders there were salaried lay officials whom the elders hired to serve the synagogue. The *hazzān* was the person in charge of the building and its furnishings. He also announced the times of service and handed the scroll to the reader and received it back from him. If there was no one else to do it, he might lead the prayers and read from the Torah. In practice he was a sacristan, master of ceremonies and teacher.[53]

Schools were located in the synagogues. Worship was understood as a means of instruction, and learning was understood as worship. Any adult person was permitted to read and preach. Women technically had this right, but were forbidden to exercise it at public services.[54] In late Judaism women were not even permitted to study Torah. Naturally persons who had spent years studying the Torah were more welcome as preachers and teachers than persons who had little education. The wise and educated preachers were called rabbis, a title of honor. In post-biblical Judaism the rabbinate developed into an ordained and salaried office.

In the synagogue tradition there were two types of religious office. That of elder was held on the basis of age and patriarchal status within the community. Because of its patriarchal nature, this office was closed to women. The office of rabbi, which was religiously the more important, was based upon learning and competence, wisdom and knowledge. Theoretically it was open to women, although its exercise was in practice closed to women by contemporary social custom and by restrictions on their access to the requisite education.

Conclusion

The tradition of priesthood had confined worship to the prescribed rituals of the cult. The tradition of the word focused worship on the hearing, understanding and living of the word of God found in scripture. The cult was concerned with the relationship of the people as a whole to God. The synagogue tradition was concerned with the religious life of the individual. The elders of Israel did at times hold political power, but they exercised it collectively. The priests held political power most of the time and exercised it hierarchically, with one individual standing at the top of the pyramid of power. Patriarchal structures existed both in the priesthood and in the office of elder. Such structures did not, however, determine the character of the offices of prophet, wisdom teacher or rabbi. The office of prophet was grounded in the call of God and exercised through the charisms of his Spirit. The office of rabbi was grounded upon individual competence and wisdom, a combination of the person's own effort of study and the gifting of God.

Thus there were two major traditions of ministry and worship in late Judaism. The one was focused on cult, the other on the word. The first related to God as object, to be moved by means of ritual. The second related to God as subject, to be listened to when he spoke to his people. The first based religious office on membership by birth in an élite caste. The second based it upon vocation and gifting by God. The first shaped its official structures on a model of hierarchy. The second followed a collective model of community.

The ministry of priesthood was completely closed to women by law. The ministry of word was at least theoretically, although not practically, open to women. Marriage was mandatory for rabbinic ordination and was considered an asset to that ministry.[55] Marriage was practiced by priests, often polygamously. Yet it remained a hindrance to cultic ministry since contact with a woman rendered the priest ritually impure and unable to participate in his cultic duties.

The ministries of priesthood and word each satisfied some of the religious needs of the people. Yet each left other needs unfulfilled. Neither tradition of ministry or worship was sufficient in itself. In post-exilic Judaism dissatisfaction with the situation and institutions of the present age led some writers to describe their hopes for an ideal age to come. Frequently these expectations took the form of the figure of a messianic king who would solve the immediate problem of political emancipation. Other writers expressed hope for the advent of an ideal prophet or priest.[56] Only one writer, Second Isaiah, described a new and unique figure, a suffering servant, who would combine in himself the functions of priest and minister of the word and at the same time transform and elevate both traditions.[57]

The two models of ministry of priesthood and word both existed during the lifetime of Jesus and were important in the contemporary religious life of Palestinian Judaism. The tradition of priesthood and cult had little influence, however, on Judaism in the diaspora. In 70

A.D. this tradition came to a definitive end even in Palestine itself. All ministry in Judaism henceforth was that of the word.

The New Testament was formed in the milieux of both Palestinian and diaspora Judaism. The evangelists drew upon earlier traditions of the life and ministry of Jesus which had originated in Palestine. But the actual written scripture of the New Testament was composed in the second half of the first century, mainly by authors coming out of various regions of the diaspora whose knowledge of Palestinian Judaism was secondhand. The next section of this chapter will explore the question of the models of ministry presented by the New Testament writers in the light of the historical background of contemporary Jewish religious offices.

MINISTRY ACCORDING TO THE NEW TESTAMENT

The Ministry of Jesus

The foundation of all Christian ministry is Jesus himself: who he is and what he said and did. The writers of the New Testament portray the ministry of Jesus in scenes of teaching and proclaiming the gospel, healing the sick, feeding the hungry, serving and self-offering in suffering and death. A theology of ministry must seek to understand Jesus in terms of his life and actions and what these mean for the shape of the ministry of his followers. It will not consider all the christological titles through which New Testament theologians sought to understand Jesus' identity. Most of these emphasized his exalted status which set him apart from ordinary persons. It will focus rather on the words and actions which the evangelists attributed to Jesus' historical life and ministry. These will be considered within the context of two great ministerial traditions of late Judaism. Then it will be necessary to ask the question whether the ministry of Jesus fit within either or both of these traditions, or whether he initiated a third new and unique form of ministry. After determining the nature of Jesus' own ministry, the subsequent section of the chapter will explore the question of which tradition of ministry became normative for Jesus' followers. Did the early Church experiment with more than one of the antecedent traditions before defining its own structures and forms of ministry? Did its final decision for the forms

of ministry within the New Testament era coincide with the character of the life and ministry of Jesus and the type of ministry he personally demanded of his followers?

Ministry of Word

All four evangelists present Jesus as a teacher. Despite the evangelists' different theological understandings of Jesus' identity they
nonetheless consistently portrayed him as a teacher, both in his own
actions and words, and in the response of those who heard him. Jesus
was commonly addressed by the people as "teacher."[58] He taught in
the synagogue on numerous occasions,[59] and also in the Temple.[60]

Like other contemporary Jewish teachers, Jesus taught the general public, but also gathered disciples around himself for a deeper
and ongoing teaching relationship. The disciples addressed Jesus as
"rabbi" or "teacher" and they are called "disciples," as were contemporary rabbinical students. Jesus is described as a "teacher of the
law,"[61] and is portrayed like the rabbis as frequently being asked
questions about the interpretation of scripture. He customarily began
his teaching with a text from scripture and then expounded upon it.[62]

As a teacher Jesus was also radically different from contemporary Jewish rabbis. He went beyond their traditional interpretation
of the Torah and proclaimed his own teaching.[63] He taught with
power and his teaching caused astonishment in his listeners.[64] He reversed some current interpretations of Torah and in one case may
even have contradicted the letter of the law.[65] Jesus also used his own
unique forms of teaching, such as the parable.

In the synoptic gospels Jesus' teaching was often associated with
a ministry of healing.[66] Frequently in miracle stories the person re-
questing Jesus' aid addressed him as "teacher."[67]

During his lifetime Jesus did not follow a systematic program
for healing all the sick people in the world. Rather he healed those
with whom he came into contact, in spontaneous compassion and on
the basis of the person's need. Such healings were exemplary, serving
as signs of who Jesus was and of how he came to serve. He did not
heal only the physical symptoms, but the whole person, in his or her
psychological, spiritual and moral dimensions as well. Jesus' minis-

try of healing was a form of ministry of the word through concrete signs of the presence and power of God's word in his gospel and in himself.

Jesus' ministry of teaching was also associated with acts of feeding the hungry. When he taught the crowds of thousands, he did not give them only ideas for their heads. The evangelists portray Jesus as aware of the deeper hunger of human beings. He gave them food for their bodies and his word which was food for the deepest longings of their hearts. He finally gave them himself at the last supper and at Calvary, the ultimate food which would heal and strengthen the whole person, giving life in the Father.

The message of Jesus' teaching is a word of life. The synoptic evangelists portray Jesus as proclaiming the advent of the kingdom of God. God's reign is already present in Jesus' own person. After his death and resurrection it will be manifested in power.[68] Jesus entrusted the mystery of the kingdom to his disciples.[69] The reign of God will bring life and salvation.[70] It may be experienced initially in the community of those who believe in Jesus. It will be experienced fully at the end of time.

The fourth evangelist developed the teaching of Jesus theologically. Jesus' teaching is presented in John as not his own, but that of the Father who sent him.[71] Jesus received it from his Father.[72] Throughout the fourth gospel Jesus is portrayed as the supreme teacher of wisdom. His work is to utter truth and to instruct men and women in the ways of God, thereby leading them to eternal life. His word demands allegiance.[73] His instruction is symbolized concretely in images of food (bread) and drink (wine and water). These are the sources of life, which satisfy the human person's deepest hunger and thirst. Jesus is more than just a wisdom teacher. He is wisdom itself. He is himself the bread and the word of life.

Thus in every aspect of his teaching Jesus went far beyond the tradition of the rabbis. He did not repeat their traditional interpretations of the Torah. He proclaimed and himself embodied a radically new torah. He proclaimed not the words of others, but the word of God which was himself. He did not only feed the minds of his listeners with instruction. He fed human persons in their wholeness, healing their brokenness and feeding them with his word of life.

Ministry of Priesthood

In the New Testament writings, with the sole exception of the Epistle to the Hebrews, there is no explicit affirmation that Jesus was a priest. Historically he was not a priest according to the norms of Judaism. However, there are hints in the synoptic gospels,[74] pauline epistles,[75] and in the johannine literature[76] that the communities which produced these writings were aware of some aspects of Jesus' life and ministry which could possibly be understood as priestly.

The only book in the New Testament in which Jesus is explicitly called "priest" and "high priest" is the Epistle to the Hebrews. Written by an unknown author and addressed to Jewish Christians, Hebrews focused the greater part of its contents on the question of the priesthood of Jesus. The epistle itself was a "word of exhortation"[77] intended to aid a community of Christians whose misunderstanding of the identity and ministry of Jesus had led to a real danger of apostasy.

Hebrews compared the priesthood of Jesus with the priesthood of Israel. It did not find them on an equal level. The epistle continually points out the superiority of Jesus' priesthood. First of all it is superior to the priesthood of Moses[78] and to that of Aaron and his descendents[79] because Jesus is the Son of God. Then the epistle presents the superiority of Jesus' priesthood to that of the whole tribe of Levi. Through Melchizedek, Jesus' priesthood was eternal and confirmed by oath.[80] The levitical priesthood was temporal and not confirmed by oath. Furthermore, the sacrifice of Jesus was offered once for all, whereas those of the levitical priests had to be repeated daily. Finally, Jesus' priesthood was superior because he himself was sinless and perfect, whereas the levitical priests had to offer sacrifice for their own sins.

The epistle next contrasted the old and the new covenants. The former was considered obsolete for it had been abrogated. Jesus' priesthood is again shown to be superior because it is based upon a new and better covenant.[81] Then the two covenant sacrifices are contrasted.[82] Jesus' sacrifice is seen as superior to those of the levitical priests first of all because he offered his own blood, not merely that of an animal. Through his offering of himself, Jesus mediated and ratified the establishment of a new covenant. Secondly, Jesus entered not only into the Holy of Holies in the Temple, but into the very presence of God in heaven. Thirdly, the sacrifice of Jesus was superior because it was offered once for all with no need of repetition.

The epistle developed these points still further in the following section.[83] Since the repeatedly offered animal sacrifices are themselves imperfect, they cannot make human beings perfect. Only the perfect sacrifice of Jesus can effect the perfection and sanctification of God's people.

The priestly functions of Christ according to the Epistle to the Hebrews are the offering of sacrifice once for all, continuing intercession for the people, and the establishment of a new covenant through his blood. Because Jesus was a priest of the new covenant, he was a new and different sort of priest. His offering of himself in sacrifice resembled not the cult of the levitical priests but the self-offering of the suffering servant. The re-establishment of the covenant was one of the functions of the suffering servant.[84] His suffering and death would heal the sins of Israel and restore the relationship of the people with their God.[85] After his sacrificial self-offering, the servant, like Jesus, would be vindicated and exalted by God.

Nowhere does the Epistle to the Hebrews connect the priesthood and sacrificial ministry of Jesus with any sort of priestly or sacrificial ministry on the part of Christians. On the contrary, it presents reasons against such a development. Jesus' priestly act of sacrifice was performed once for all and abolished any need for further sacrifice. The present ministry of Jesus, according to Hebrews, is one of intercession. The new covenant is one of promise and inheritance which elicits a response of love and righteous conduct.[86] It is not a covenant of cult, of sacrificial ritual or of observance of regulations.[87] Nowhere does Hebrews propose Old Testament priesthood as a model for Christian ministry. The type of ministry suggested by Hebrews is rather one of healing, peacemaking, sanctification, exhortation, love, hospitality and care of prisoners and outcasts.[88]

Ministry of Service

In the Old Testament the phrase "servant of the Lord" is profoundly rich in connotative meaning. It was applied to all the great religious heroes: the patriarchs, Moses, David, the prophets and the wise man Job. It denotes a righteous Israelite, one who kept the covenant of the Lord. It frequently formed part of the confession of faith and humility of the good person calling him/herself "your servant" when standing before God in prayer.[89]

The word "servant" in Hebrew means one who does work for another or who belongs to another like a slave. It also meant one who was committed to another in loyal allegiance, as the soldiers or ministers of the king. The word "service" in Hebrew had the further meaning of cultic worship. The "servant of the Lord" was thus a person who stood faithful to God in worship and prayer. Finally, the Lord's servant was the person who lived in faithful obedience to his covenant.[90]

The title "servant of the Lord" is used with special significance in Second Isaiah. In the book as a whole, outside of the servant songs, the phrase denotes the whole people Israel. Yahweh has created his servant, chosen and called him. God asked the servant only to trust him and promised the gift of his help.

In the servant songs, which are distinct from, yet closely related to the other parts of Second Isaiah, the figure of the servant has also been understood collectively. Yet the second servant song[91] portrays both the servant and God speaking about a mission of the servant to Israel. This passage presents the greatest obstacle to a collective understanding of the servant, for it is difficult to see how the same figure can represent both Israel and God's minister to Israel.[92] Some interpreters of these passages from the intertestamental period on through the centuries have understood the servant as an individual and some have even identified the servant with the messiah.[93]

The servant songs draw a vivid portrait of the servant of the Lord. The servant has been formed by Yahweh from the womb, chosen, called and solemnly named by God who endowed the servant with his own Holy Spirit.[94] Righteous and innocent, he would bear the sins of the people. He would suffer violence, humiliation and rejection. Finally, he would be put to death, offering his life for the salvation of the people.[95]

The ministry of the servant was to serve Yahweh and the people Israel and ultimately also the gentiles. It was to serve those who most needed but did not necessarily merit help. This service was to be accomplished in several ways. The ministry of the servant was first of all the proclamation of God's word of justice.[96] In Second Isaiah the establishment of God's justice was connected with the historical restoration of Israel. In the servant songs this meaning was extended so that the servant was called to mediate God's truth, righteousness and salvation as a light to the nations.[97]

The second ministerial function of the servant in these passages was to suffer. The servant accepted suffering voluntarily and made it an offering and an intercession for the sin of the people. His suffering would effect the healing of the people from their sins and their restoration to wholeness. This suffering would culminate in the death of the servant. Yet he would ultimately be vindicated by Yahweh before all the kings and peoples of the earth.[98]

In the Old Testament and the intertestamental literature the servant of the Lord was sometimes identified with the messiah.[99] However, none of these texts goes so far as to suggest that the servant as messiah would suffer.[100] There was a basic dichotomy in late Judaism between the expectation of a victorious king-messiah who would restore the national and earthly glory of Israel, and the humble and obscure figure of the suffering servant.

In the New Testament the title "servant" with a personal pronoun connecting it to God was applied to Jesus five times: at his baptism, twice in Peter's sermon in Acts, and twice in the response of Peter's friends.[101] All of these passages are from early strata of tradition.

The servant songs of Second Isaiah are explicitly cited six times in the New Testament.[102] The influence of the songs on New Testament christology is however much greater. Implicit references to the servant songs are found in pre-pauline,[103] pre-synoptic,[104] and early johannine tradition.[105] Servant references appear in the archaic confessional and liturgical formulae which are much older than the written epistles and gospels. Thus the servant understanding of Jesus seems to have been important in the very earliest christological tradition of the New Testament.

Three elements in the synoptic account of Jesus' baptism are related to the first servant song:[106] the phrases "son," "beloved" and "well pleased." Matthew described Jesus' ministry of preaching and healing in terms of two Isaian passages which reflect the theology of servant.[107] According to Cullman,[108] all three synoptic gospels and Paul present Jesus in the role of the servant in the last supper accounts. Underlying the passion predictions there may also be a veiled reference to Isaiah 53. The title "lamb" in the baptism narrative in John, when understood through its Aramaic equivalent which means both "lamb" and "servant" is generally accepted as another designation of Jesus as the servant.[109] In Acts it was by showing the identity of Jesus as the servant of Isaiah 53 that Philip effected the conversion of the Ethiopian.[110]

It is not possible to know for certain whether Jesus understood himself as the suffering servant of Second Isaiah. The synoptic evangelists portray Jesus speaking about himself in the imagery of servant theology.[111] Such sayings stem from early, pre-synoptic tradition. It is possible that they do represent actual sayings of Jesus. This cannot, however, be known for certain. In these passages the evangelists present Jesus explicitly connecting his own servanthood with the nature of discipleship which he expected of his followers.[112] "Whoever would be great among you must be your servant."[113]

What is evident from the New Testament is that the suffering servant of the Lord was an important image through which the primitive Christian community sought to understand Jesus' identity and ministry. The early servant christology was later eclipsed by other christological images, perhaps because the humble figure of the servant seemed less than adequate to the christology of the gentile church which preferred to portray Jesus as the son of God and the exalted and glorified Lord.

The servant according to the Old Testament was, like the prophet, called and chosen by God and gifted with his charisms and with his Spirit. The servant was also, like the prophet, commissioned to proclaim the word of the Lord. Both the servant and the prophet confidently expected that even if their efforts were a failure in the eyes of the world they would ultimately be vindicated by God. Like the priest the servant represented the people before God and offered sacrifice.[114] Thus the ministry of the servant was a ministry of both word and sacrifice. Yet it transcended the ministry of prophet and priest because the servant ultimately offered himself, his own suffering and death, as word and sacrifice, thereby bringing the salvation of the Lord.

The ministry of the servant as presented in the New Testament is a combination of service of the word and of priesthood. Yet it also transcended both. The servant served the Lord and his people.[115] He served by proclamation of the word and by himself being the word. He served by feeding the hungry, healing the broken, suffering and dying.[116] Jesus' own ministry of service was presented in the New Testament as a primary model for the ministry of his followers.[117]

The ministry of the servant in the Old Testament was rooted in his relationship with God and in the gifting of the Holy Spirit. The foundation of Jesus' own ministry lay in his relationship to his Father and its manifestation in continuous personal prayer. For Jesus as for his followers the source of ministry is not the self, but God. Ministry is possible only insofar as the minister's life is rooted in deep personal relationship to God.

In the New Testament there are strong traditions of Jesus' prayer. The evangelists attest to the importance of prayer in the life of Jesus by the great number of times they portray Jesus praying. For Jesus prayer was both a private act[118] and a communal one. Jesus regularly attended public worship in the synagogue where he also ministered himself by preaching and healing.[119] He also sought privacy and solitude for prayer.[120] The traditions of his private prayer are strongest in Luke[121] where Jesus is portrayed as habitually praying at moments of importance and decision.[122] Five independent traditions bear witness to Jesus' prayer in Gethsemane at this great moment of crisis.[123] Jesus prayed also during his final moments on the cross.[124]

Jesus' teaching on prayer is found in all four strands of synoptic tradition.[125] He strongly urged his followers to approach God in prayer and to expect God to hear and answer their prayers.[126] He taught them to come together in groups to pray, as well as to pray individually.[127] Finally he taught them how to pray: Abba, Father.[128]

Jesus related to God in a special way as son to his Father. Yet he taught his followers also to relate to God as their Father. As children of the same Father, he proclaimed them his own brothers and sisters.

Jesus' relationship to God as son is linked with the image of his anointing by the Holy Spirit in the gospel scenes of his baptism.[129] In the course of his ministry Jesus continually experienced the power of the Spirit in his acts of healing and exorcism.[130]

The character of Jesus' own life and ministry stand as an example for his followers. Christian life and servant ministry must fundamentally be rooted in deep personal relationship with God. This

relationship is manifested both in prayer which is frequent and sometimes even constant, and also in the presence and gifts of the Holy
Spirit.

Conclusion

The ministry of Jesus was a ministry of both word and sacrifice.
Yet it was a ministry which far transcended the functions of the rabbi and priest. His ministry was a ministry of service, service of gratuitous self-offering in suffering and even death for the salvation of the
people. Jesus came to serve: to serve his Father and all the people.
His service was manifested in many forms: teaching and healing,
proclaiming the gospel and feeding the hungry, suffering and dying.
His service effected the restoration of men and women to wholeness
before God.

The primary Old Testament image through which the writers of
the New Testament understood Jesus' ministry was that of the suffering servant of Second Isaiah. Some New Testament writers did
also portray Jesus as priest, but with important qualifications. His
priesthood was radically different from that of the levitical priests
and his once-for-all sacrifice of himself abolished the need for any
continuation of priesthood or cult of the levitical model. In short, Jesus' priesthood resembled that of the suffering servant, not that of
the temple priests.

The evangelists also presented Jesus as a rabbi, but here too the
image was qualified. Jesus was not bound to the rabbinic tradition of
legal interpretation. In total freedom he preached God's reign, in
comparison to which the law was of subordinate importance and
might even be put aside when it stood in the way of God's working in
love.

Thus Jesus united in himself the great ministerial traditions of
Judaism through the image of the servant. At the same time he transformed these traditions and gave them new meaning. The words and
actions of Jesus as presented by the four evangelists provide the concrete basis for a model of Christian ministry. Jesus was himself a servant, and he instructed his followers also to be servants. He
ministered to the deepest needs of the people, healing their brokenness, satisfying their hunger and thirst for God, restoring them to
wholeness in their humanity. His own life and ministry were ground-

ed in his relationship to his Father and in the presence and gifts of the Holy Spirit. Jesus called men and women to follow him and to live and serve as he had lived and served.

Ministry During the Lifetime of Jesus: Discipleship

While Jesus himself was yet living and ministering on this earth, he began to send forth other persons to minister also. This was the beginning of Christian ministry. What was the nature of this earliest form of ministry during Jesus' own lifetime? It was determined by Jesus himself: who he was, how he himself ministered, his call to follow him and his sending forth. Jesus did not establish structural offices, much less a hierarchy of offices. Nor did he ordain. There is no mention of a Christian priesthood either during the lifetime of Jesus or in the New Testament Church.

There is only one title used in the New Testament to describe the ministry of Jesus' followers before the resurrection: discipleship. Jesus called men and women to follow him and become his disciples. Those persons whom he called left their previous occupations and possessions, followed Jesus and became his disciples. What precisely did it mean to be a "disciple"? In the New Testament discipleship of Jesus is presented within the framework of ministry of word. However, this is qualified as, more importantly, ministry of service. The Christian disciple differs from the rabbinic disciple precisely because (s)he is called to be God's servant, just as the master, Jesus, was himself servant.

In the ancient Mediterranean world, the concept of discipleship originated in the Greek philosophical schools.[131] The Hebrew and Greek words for "disciple" are not found in the Hebrew Old Testament or in the Septuagint. The Old Testament prophets seem to have avoided the image of the teacher-disciple relationship.[132] Instead they pointed to God as sole teacher and human persons as disciples of God.[133] There was little veneration of persons or of tradition in the Old Testament in comparison to what developed later in the rabbinic schools. In the Old Testament God was presented as revealing his word more or less directly to his people.

In the Greek philosophical schools disciples served and imitated their teachers as well as learned from them. This concept of discipleship influenced Judaism in the hellenistic period. The first mention of a distinct class of wisdom teachers in Judaism occurred in Ben Sira which was written in the early second century B.C. shortly before the Maccabean revolt when hellenistic influence on Palestinian Judaism was intense.[134] Ben Sira himself presided over a scribal school in Jerusalem.

In the Greek and Roman periods these scribal schools grew and developed into rabbinical schools. The rabbis dedicated their lives to the study of the Torah. Rabbis who were members of the Pharisee party at the time of Jesus called themselves "disciples of Moses."[135] Rabbinic teachers required of their disciples learning of the Torah itself and also of the rabbi's own interpretation of the Torah. Service of and submission to the teacher were also expected of rabbinic disciples. In the first century, schools of rabbinic interpretation were developing in which tradition was formally handed down from master to disciple. When the disciple had mastered the tradition of his teacher, then he in turn was ordained a rabbi and began to teach and to acquire disciples in his own right. The discipleship of Paul to Rabbi Gamaliel is described in Acts.[136] In the first century women were not permitted to study Torah in the rabbinic schools.

In the New Testament Jesus was addressed as "rabbi" by his own disciples and by outsiders. He taught, interpreted scripture and had disciples. There were, however, major differences between the mode of discipleship required by Jesus and that of the rabbinical schools. In the first place, Jesus himself personally called at least some of his disciples.[137] The rabbis usually waited until disciples came to them. The disciples called by Jesus lacked appropriate qualifications for rabbinic discipleship, such as learning and strict observance of the law. They were instead unlettered fishermen and public sinners. According to the fourth gospel, the disciples were given to Jesus by his Father.[138] Some disciples did, however, come to Jesus on their own initiative.[139]

The disciples of Jesus were committed to his person[140] instead of just to his teaching as were rabbinic disciples. This commitment was total and exclusive.[141] Jesus demanded radical detachment from all else and radical obedience to himself, rather than to the Torah.[142] Discipleship of Jesus was a permanent state, to be lived until death. It was not, like rabbinic discipleship, a temporary stage on the way to becoming a rabbi. Jesus called his disciples to share in his present work and suffering.[143] It was not necessary to wait until they had successfully completed their term of discipleship. Jesus also called his disciples to share in his own servanthood which culminated in gratuitous suffering and death. They were not asked, like the rabbinic disciples, to serve their teacher during their period of discipleship and then to subject others to serve them. The relationship between Jesus and his disciples was unique within Judaism and Hellenism. It was determined by who Jesus was and by his own self-awareness.[144] Jesus related to his disciples not as rabbi but as lord and as servant.

In the call narratives of all four gospels Jesus is portrayed calling persons to follow him. When the persons heard the call, they left their previous existence and followed Jesus. The following of Jesus required detachment from anyone or anything other than him.

The synoptic gospels present some of the teaching of Jesus on the subject of discipleship. The disciples must love no one more than Jesus.[145] They must give away all possessions.[146] They must be willing to embrace suffering and even death for Jesus.[147] They must become as children and servants.[148] Yet in their discipleship they will be blessed by God more than the greatest of other human persons.[149] In their suffering and persecution they can rely on the Spirit of God to help them, and upon God to save and vindicate them in the end.[150] John 17 presents the prayer of Jesus for his disciples, entrusting them to his Father as he entrusted the Father's word to them, and praying that the Father's love may be in them and that Jesus himself remain present to them.

What were the tasks of the disciple of Jesus according to the New Testament evangelists? The first task was the preaching of the gospel.[151] This involved proclaiming Jesus' message about the reign of God[152] and bearing witness to the inbreaking of the kingdom in the person of Jesus.[153] Through their preaching mission the disciples were instructed to make disciples of all people.[154]

The second task of the disciple of Jesus was healing. The disciples were sent to heal the sick[155] and to exorcise demons which might cause physical or mental illnesses.[156] Finally they were sent to heal through the forgiveness of sins.[157] Physical healing and forgiveness of sins had been connected in the ministry of Jesus as portrayed by the synoptic evangelists.[158] These ministries were later extended to the disciples.

The disciples of Jesus were explicitly commissioned to the ministries of preaching and healing in the synoptic gospels. They were implicitly commissioned to a third ministry: feeding the hungry. Mark portrayed Jesus as having the disciples share in the work of feeding the multitude.[159] In the parallel story of the multiplication of the loaves Jesus commanded the disciples to feed the people: "You give them something to eat."[160] In the johannine version of the story Jesus told the disciples to gather up the fragments after the meal was over. In the following discourse on the bread of life Jesus is portrayed by the fourth evangelist as calling the food the bread of eternal life which is his own flesh, given for the life of the world.[161]

The final task of the disciple was to serve. The disciple was expected to serve as his master served, in total self-offering even to the giving up of one's life.[162] In Matthew 23 Jesus is portrayed as addressing his disciples and contrasting their mode of discipleship with that of the scribes and pharisees:

> As to you, avoid the title "Rabbi." One among you is your teacher, the rest are learners. Do not call anyone on earth your father. Only one is your father, the One in heaven. Avoid being called teachers. Only one is your teacher, the Messiah. The greatest among you will be the one who serves the rest. Whoever exalts himself shall be humbled, but whoever humbles himself shall be exalted.[163]

Thus contemporary rabbinic understanding of discipleship was radically altered by Jesus, precisely through the application of the connotations of the suffering servant of the Lord. This is the closest the New Testament comes to a definition of Jesus' own understanding and teaching about the nature of ministry. Jesus formed and sent forth disciples to minister as he himself ministered, that is, as servants who were ready to embrace suffering and even death as part of their ministry.

Who were the disciples of Jesus? They are variously described as "the Twelve" and "the Seventy (or seventy-two)" and as a great multitude. There are stories in the New Testament of the call of the Twelve[164] and of the commissioning of these men by Jesus.[165] But these are not the only official disciples. There are also accounts of the commissioning of the Seventy by Jesus.[166] The Seventy were given the same mission of proclaiming the gospel and healing the sick.[167] It was stated that those who heard the Seventy heard Jesus, and those who rejected them rejected Jesus.[168] The disciples of Jesus were also referred to as a "great number."[169] Many disciples were named in the gospels who were not members of the Twelve: Nathanael, Nicodemus, Joseph of Arimathea.[170] It is among this larger group of disciples, perhaps identical with the Seventy, that a number of women were found. Luke described the Twelve and the women disciples sharing in the ministry of Jesus in Galilee.[171] He named Mary of Magdala, Joanna the wife of Chuza, and Susanna, and mentioned that there were also many other women who served.

Ministries of the Early Church

a. **The Office of Apostle.** The word "apostle" means "one sent forth." The institution may derive from the Jewish office of the *shā-lîah.*[172] This was an official emissary, commissioned and sent forth by the Sanhedrin or later by the Jewish high council at Jamnia. Such emissaries were usually sent out in pairs to collect tithes and resolve disputes on religious questions and to proclaim religious truths. They were commissioned for their task by the imposition of hands. When acting within the limits of their specific mission, they possessed the authority of the body which had sent them. They were given letters of accreditation verifying their authority and mission. In Judaism such officials were not, however, missionaries and did not attempt to make converts.

In the New Testament in the Epistle to the Hebrews Jesus himself was called *apostolos,* the one sent by the Father.[173] John 20:21 connects the sending of Jesus by the Father with Jesus' own sending of his followers: "As the Father has sent me, even so do I send you." However, the two are not totally analogous. Jesus was sent as God's own son, as a sign of his divine glory, and as judgment to those who accept or reject him. The followers of Jesus are fallible human persons who are sent to bear witness to the good news of his life, death and resurrection.

Historically, the office of apostle arose after the resurrection out of the groups of disciples who had been associated with Jesus during his lifetime. On the basis of their faith in his resurrection the disciples were commissioned by the risen Jesus to proclaim his gospel, to heal the sick and feed the hungry. Through the example of their lives they were to bear witness to the crucified and risen Jesus.[174]

All four gospels portray Jesus sending forth his disciples as witnesses to his resurrection.[175] It is only after the resurrection that these persons are called "apostles."[176] In the writings of Paul the term "apostle" denotes a person who had seen the risen Christ and been commissioned by him.[177] Luke added a third condition in Acts, that the apostle had accompanied Jesus throughout his historical ministry.[178] This criterion disqualified Paul and most of the missionary apostles. In the fourth gospel John connected Jesus' commissioning of his followers with their reception of the Holy Spirit.[179]

In the first decade after the resurrection the apostolate was closely associated and sometimes identified with the institution of the Twelve, although there were other apostles in Jerusalem and Judaea. Later the understanding of apostolate was expanded to include missionary apostles. The apostleship of both groups was grounded upon the same two basic criteria of having seen and been commissioned by the risen Jesus.

When the first generation of eyewitnesses who had accompanied Jesus during his ministry and had witnessed his post-resurrectional appearances died out, there was no one who could then qualify for the office of apostle. By its very definition, requiring personal witness of and commissioning by the risen Jesus, the office of apostle prepared for its own demise. After the death of the Twelve, there were other apostles in the Church for a time, especially the missionary apostles. But after the end of the period of the founding of churches in the various cities and provinces of the Roman empire, missionary apostles also disappeared from the scene. Responsibility for the leadership and administration of the churches passed from the apostles to local leaders. It was from the offices of these local leaders, which varied in form from place to place, and not from the institution of the apostolate, that the later structural offices of the Church developed.

b. The Twelve. Much of the current controversy about the nature of ministry in the Church and the role of women in ministry is due to a misunderstanding of the institution of the Twelve. The

Twelve were distinct from the other apostles, but they were definitely not the only apostles. They had a very specific theological function in the nascent Church, although the historical role of individual members of the Twelve was not very different from that of other apostles.

All four gospels and Acts mention the Twelve.[180] In the synoptic gospels and Acts they are named in three groups of four. The groups remain stable in all the lists, although there are variations among the names in the second and third groups. According to Mark, Jesus himself chose the members of the Twelve.[181] There is no question that many of the Twelve, and all of the first group, were close companions of Jesus during his ministry. During the lifetime of Jesus they were called disciples.[182] Only one passage in the New Testament portrayed Jesus himself using the term "apostle" but the reference there was to the future.[183] After the resurrection the disciples were uniformly called apostles.

The Twelve played a special role immediately after the resurrection. They symbolically represented the twelve tribes of Israel. As such the role of the Twelve was to symbolize the completeness of the new people of God at two important moments: at Pentecost, which was the beginning of the Church, and at the eschaton which would mark the end of the Church as an historical institution. For this reason it was theologically necessary for the Eleven to reconstitute their number to twelve by the election of Matthias to replace Judas. This was done immediately before Pentecost, so that the new people of God would be symbolically complete at the moment when the Church was born. After Pentecost it was no longer important that there be twelve historical persons, and the members were not replaced after their death.[184]

It was because of this symbolic function of representing the completeness of Israel that the members of the Twelve were all men.[185] According to the tradition of Judaism, Israel was legally constituted by its male members. Thus the male character of the members of the Twelve had to do with the theological symbolism of that temporary institution, not with the ministry of the Church. After the Church had expanded far beyond Judaism, such symbolism had less and less importance. Nowhere does the New Testament indicate any handing down of this symbolic, and therefore male, role of the

Twelve to others in the Church. Nor is there any evidence that other offices or ministries in the time of Jesus and the earliest decades of the Church were limited to men.

After the resurrection, the community of Christians which gathered in the upper room in Jerusalem to await the coming of the Spirit was composed of three groups: the Eleven, the women and the family of Jesus.[186] The group of women were those who had been present at the crucifixion and who had been witnesses of the resurrection appearances. The name most often mentioned by the evangelists from this group was Mary of Magdala. It is probable that she was their leader.[187] The family of Jesus also included at least one woman, his mother.

After Pentecost some members of the Twelve, and especially Peter, played an important leadership role in the primitive Church.[188] The authority of Peter was acknowledged by Paul in the early years of his own ministry.[189] It is not certain that the Twelve as an institution ever exercised administrative authority, although some of its members did individually.[190]

The authority of the Twelve disappeared altogether in the Church after the death of its members. After Pentecost the original members were not and theologically could not be replaced. James, son of Zebedee, was martyred under Herod Agrippa in the early 40's.[191] As early as Paul's first visit as a Christian to Jerusalem,[192] the leaders of the Jerusalem church were Peter and James, the brother of Jesus, who was not a member of the Twelve. By the time of the council of Jerusalem the administration of the church of Jerusalem consisted of "apostles and elders" of whom James, the brother of Jesus, was the recognized leader and spokesperson.[193] Thus within a decade after the resurrection the leadership of the Jerusalem church was already passing to persons outside the institution of the Twelve.

The authority of the Twelve and of the Judean apostles was connected in part with their location at Jerusalem. In the beginning Jerusalem was the heart of the Christian community. But this situation soon changed. As early as the martyrdom of Stephen, many Christians of the Jerusalem community were scattered "throughout the region of Judaea and Samaria."[194] The apostles remained in the city at that time, but meanwhile other churches were being founded and growing to maturity in the more important cities of the empire, such as Antioch, Corinth, Ephesus and Rome. During the Jewish war of 66–73 A.D. the Christian community left Jerusalem altogether and did not return in any significant numbers until centuries later. The institution of the Twelve did not reappear in any other city, since its membership could only be constituted by eyewitnesses, most of whom by that time had died, and since its authority was grounded in its symbolism which had no further theological relevance until the eschaton. In the other cities of the empire new forms of leadership and authority were developing which were completely independent of the institution of the Twelve.

The New Testament passage which is generally cited as a basis for the theological doctrine of apostolic succession, understood as a transmission of office in a quasi-physical sense, is Acts 6. Acts 6:2 is the only mention of the Twelve in the entire book. The contextual situation of the passage is a dispute between factions of hebrew and hellenist Christians. The Twelve are not portrayed as deciding the dispute themselves, but as summoning the larger community of apostles to resolve it collegially.

Seven hellenists were chosen to minister to their own community. The apostles, not exclusively the Twelve, prepared them for this new mission through prayer and the imposition of hands. This was not ordination as it is generally understood today. Ordination denotes incorporation into an order. It presupposes first that a concretely defined official order already exists and secondly that those administering ordination are themselves members of or incorporated into the same order. A number of passages in the New Testament mention the practice of laying on of hands, but in none of these does it denote ordination. The latter did not develop into an official practice in the Church until post-biblical times. In the New Testament the role of laying on of hands is by no means limited to apostles. In Acts 13 it was the prophets and teachers of the church of Antioch who laid hands on Paul and Barnabas, blessing them for a new mission. Later on in the pastoral epistles reference was made to the gifts of the Spirit which Timothy had received earlier in his life when the council of elders had laid hands upon him.[195]

Thus Acts 6 may not be understood as proof that the Twelve transmitted their office to successors through the laying on of hands. On the contrary, the Seven seem to have been chosen for a new and different ministry, not for a continuation of the apostolic office. Apart from this passage there is no other evidence in the New Testament that the apostolic office was transmitted to successors. What was handed down were the apostolic functions and tradition. A pre-pauline confessional formula in 1 Corinthians 15 traced the transmission of tradition not only from the Twelve, but also from James and the other apostles. Thus the authority of Christian tradition is preserved not through the continuation of the office of the Twelve, but through continuity with the eyewitness generation who had personally received the tradition from Jesus himself.

　　c. **Missionary Apostles.** It was the missionary element which distinguished the Christian apostolate from the otherwise similar Jewish office of emissary. Christian apostles were sent forth to witness to the risen Christ "to the ends of the earth."[196] The primary work of the apostles was the proclamation of the gospel in order to effect conversions and found churches.

　　Paul was the missionary apostle *par excellence* and also the one about whom the most information is known. He too was commissioned by the risen Jesus, although after the close of the period of resurrection appearances as such. His apostolate was confirmed by other apostles and by the church of Antioch.[197]

　　The missionary apostle was, according to Paul, a person set apart as the representative or ambassador of Christ.[198] As such the task of the apostle was to proclaim to the people the saving words and actions of God in Jesus. The apostle was both co-worker with Christ and, like him, a servant.[199] For Paul the authority of the apostle existed for the building up of the Church in love and for bearing witness to the world of the love of God in Jesus.[200]

　　Paul further understood his own apostleship in terms of preaching the cross of Jesus, correcting moral abuses, reconciling people to God and guiding the Church. Paul described his own apostolic ministry as taking place through a combination of hard work and divine grace.[201] For Paul the fact of being sent on a mission as witness to the risen Christ was the essential element of apostleship. But the imitation of the death and resurrection of Jesus in his own life was also an important task of the apostle.[202]

　　A theological understanding of the ministry of the apostle began to be developed in the letters of Paul. Paul first described the ministry of Jesus as that of servant.[203] He wrote of his own ministry in terms of being the "servant of Christ."[204] In the authentic pauline letters the words "service" (*diakonia*), "servant" and the verb "to serve" are used more than twenty times to describe Paul's own apostolic ministry.[205] Yet the meaning of *diakonia* is not strictly limited to apostolic service. In Ephesians 4:12 it is applied to the ministries of apostles, prophets, evangelists, pastors and teachers. All are forms of service. All serve to build up the community of Christ's body.

The imitation of Jesus in service and in suffering was one of Paul's greatest ideals But it was an ideal which he lived in his own ministry, serving real human persons and communities more than structures or ideologies. He believed that the true test of authenticity of apostolic ministry was whether the apostle imitated Jesus in his service of suffering.[206] The authority of the apostolic office derived from the authentic imitation of Jesus in suffering service. It was the antithesis of hierarchical authority. It was not imposed from above through the exercise of power, but came from below, from humble service. This service was exercised collegially with other servants of Jesus, respecting the equality and freedom of other human persons.[207] Through the exercise of this type of authority the apostle was able to elicit true and lasting conversion-commitments to Jesus.

The Judean apostles, as presented by Luke-Acts, were historical companions of Jesus. Their role and authority were concerned with guaranteeing the tradition of Jesus handed down through them. It was on this basis that they resolved new questions which arose. The authority of the missionary apostle, on the other hand, was based upon his or her knowledge and experience of the risen Christ. Out of this understanding of the death and resurrection of Jesus and their implications for Christian life, the missionary apostle drew data by means of which to decide new issues. For this reason the missionary apostles tended to be more innovative than their Judean counterparts.[208]

As primarily the founders of churches, the missionary apostles' role diminished as the churches grew and developed independent lives of their own. The missionary apostles were gradually replaced by the indigenous leaders of the churches they had founded. After the deaths of the original missionary apostles who could claim to have been personally commissioned by the risen Christ, the apostolic office as such disappeared from the Church. There is no evidence that the missionary apostles, any more than the Twelve or the other Judean apostles made any attempt to transmit their own office to successors. Although there is evidence of the transmission of apostolic function and tradition, there is no traceable succession of office from the Twelve or the apostles to the presbyters and bishops who emerged as the leaders of local churches later in the first century.[209]

Ministry of Priesthood

There is no evidence in the New Testament for the existence of a ministerial office of priesthood in the earliest Christian Church. The title "priest" in the New Testament was applied only to Jesus himself, to the Jewish temple priests, and to the whole Christian people.[210]

In the Epistle to the Hebrews Jesus was presented as the eternal high priest whose once-for-all sacrifice of himself had abolished any further need for a cultic, levitical type of priesthood. Some have used this fact to explain the absence of Christian priests elsewhere in the New Testament. Raymond Brown has criticized this procedure as illegitimate since it deduces a general principal applying to the New Testament as a whole from the theology of one epistle which was itself relatively isolated and late and had little influence on other New Testament writings.[211]

Hebrews does proclaim the priesthood of Jesus, but a priesthood of a new and different order, a priesthood like that of the suffering servant. It does not make any connection between Jesus' own priesthood and any sort of priestly ministry on the part of Christians.

The four texts in the New Testament which proclaim the priesthood of the whole Christian people have been understood by some, including Luther, to mean that if all are priests, then no official priestly office is necessary.[212] This assumption is also open to question. All of these texts are based on Exodus 19:6. John H. Elliott has shown that the purpose of this text was to describe the holiness of the people.[213] Because of their covenant relationship with Yahweh the people are to be as holy as priests. This does not imply that they are to function as cultic priests. The Exodus text stands almost immediately before the account of the institution of the levitical priesthood at Sinai. It was never viewed as precluding it. The texts about the priesthood of the Christian people in the New Testament do not give any information about the development of the office of priest in the Church, which occurred after the close of the New Testament period, or about the appropriateness of such a development.

There is only one text in the New Testament which might indicate the beginning of an understanding of Christian ministry as priestly. In Romans 15:16 Paul wrote: "The grace given to me by God to be a minister (*leitourgos*) of Christ Jesus to the gentiles in the priestly service (*leitourgounta*) of the gospel of God, so that the offering (*prosphora*) of the gentiles may be acceptable, sanctified (*hagiasmenos*) by the Holy Spirit." This description of Paul's own ministry of word in cultic terminology was written for the purpose of supporting his authority to criticize and exhort members of the Roman church in the finer points of Christian living. However, Paul's primary office and title was that of apostle. His own descriptions of his ministry are always in terms of ministry of the word and of service, not of cult. Paul did baptize, but did not reserve this function to himself or to apostles in general. On the contrary he argued that it should not be the task of missionary apostles.[214] His own ministry was primarily concerned with proclamation of the gospel and witness to Jesus in suffering service. Romans 15:16 indicates that priestly connotations were not thought of, at least by Paul, as completely incompatible with Christian ministry of word and service. However, in Paul's understanding ministry was a much larger concept of which the cultic or priestly was only a minor part. Ministry for Paul was service, service like that of Jesus', a service which was authenticated through suffering.

In the early years of the Church, Christians continued to recognize the Jewish priesthood and to participate in temple worship.[215] Brown has suggested that a Christian priesthood could not develop until the Church had broken off from Judaism and acquired a self-identity as a distinct religion, and until it had developed its own sacrificial cult for which the presence of priests was required.[216] The first condition occurred after the Second Temple had been destroyed and the Christian movement excommunicated from the synagogue (circa A.D. 85). The eucharist began to be understood as a cultic sacrifice toward the end of the first century.[217] The role of presiding at the eucharist had, of course, existed much earlier and been exercised by

various ministers. It is Brown's thesis that Christian priesthood did
not develop directly out of any one office in the New Testament, but
emerged as a combination of several different offices or ministries,
especially those of disciple, apostle, presbyter-bishop and presider at
the eucharist.[218] This does not, however, account for the levitical
character of the Christian priesthood in later centuries. It is perhaps
more accurate to say that Christian ministry in general emerged out
of the convergence of various New Testament forms of ministry,
whereas Christian priesthood as a structural institution was molded
by the second-century rediscovery of the model of levitical priesthood.

Ministry of Service

a. The Meaning of Diakonia in the New Testament. In hellenistic Greek the basic meaning of the word *diakonia* is service. This service often took the form of service at table. In Greek culture no form
of service was desirable or meaningful. In the Old Testament and semitic culture, on the other hand, service was honorable in proportion
to the greatness of the master served.

In the New Testament *diakonia* denotes service and is synony-
mous with ministry. It is used in two ways: one general, of all Christian ministry, and in the later writings in a narrower sense referring
to a specific office within the Church, that of the diaconate.

All *diakonia* ultimately derives from Jesus' own ministry as servant. Paul called Jesus a *diakonos,* or servant, of the Jewish people.[219]
The synoptic gospels proclaimed service as the purpose for which Jesus came.[220] They also explicitly linked Jesus' own ministry of service
with the nature of ministry he expected of his disciples.[221] The ultimate form of service for Jesus and for his followers would be total
self-emptying in offering one's life for others.[222]

In the New Testament the basic ministry of service is the following of Jesus, becoming his disciple.[223] This general form of *diakonia* is
further described as service of the word,[224] of witness to the gospel,[225]
as service of reconciliation,[226] service of the new covenant,[227] service
of the gospel,[228] service of Christ's body, the Church,[229] service of
alms for those who are in need,[230] and service of healing and discern-
ment.[231] Paul emphasized the obvious point: there are many varieties
of service.[232]

Paul uses the term *diakonos,* meaning "minister" or "servant," several times to describe his own ministry,[233] although his principal title was apostle. He used the term also of his co-workers.[234] He described service as a gift given by the risen Christ through the Holy Spirit to those whom he has chosen for his service.[235]

The narrower meaning of *diakonia* denotes a specific office within the Church. This office first appeared in the churches of the diaspora as early as the mid-fifties.[236] The New Testament gives little information either on the origins of the diaconate or of the functions of this office. It is certain that by the time of the pastoral epistles, near the end of the first century, the diaconate was a formally established office within the Church.

b. The Office of Deacon. The story of the seven in Acts 6:1–6 has often been called the "institution of the diaconate." This understanding is problematic for several reasons. The contextual situation of the passage was that there had been a conflict in the early Jerusalem church between hellenist and hebrew Christians over the question of whether the widows of the hellenist community were receiving their just due of alms money. Pressured by the necessity of dealing with such questions, the Twelve, acting collegially with the other apostles, appointed seven hellenists to serve, presumably by distributing alms to the widows of their community. The apostles blessed and commissioned them for this new ministry by prayer and the imposition of hands. This passage has often been understood as the basis for the rite of ordination. Yet what is described is not ordination in the later technical sense, of incorporation into an order, but blessing and commissioning.[237] There is no evidence that the Seven were being installed into an existing office or incorporated into the order of those who commissioned them. In fact, it is not at all clear from this passage exactly to what sort of ministry they were being commissioned. It was explicitly stated that this ministry was intended to be different from that of the apostles commissioning them.

There is a further problem that the actual ministry of the Seven according to other texts in Acts was not limited to the distribution of alms to hellenist widows. Two of the Seven, Stephen and Philip, were portrayed as exercising a ministry of proclamation and miracles. In the case of Stephen it is possible that he was already engaged in a preaching ministry before the commission to alms distribution, since at that time it was noted that he was already full of faith and of the Holy Spirit.[238] Philip is presented at a later time in a ministry of evangelism and was called by the title "evangelist."[239] Raymond Brown has suggested that the Seven were originally the leaders of the hellenist community and as such were more comparable to the later office of bishop than to that of deacon. Luke, writing in the 80's may have viewed the apostles as bishops and may have been seeking in this passage to portray the hellenist leaders in a subordinate position.[240]

Thus Acts 6 does not give evidence of the institution of the office of deacon in the Church. It is not certain whether the ministry for which the Seven were chosen had any real relationship to the later ecclesiastical office of deacon. The passage does show that at a rather early time in the New Testament period distinctions between different types and forms of ministry were being made. It also gives evidence of the use of prayer, blessing and the laying on of hands for the purpose of commissioning persons to new ministries.

The diaconate as an official ecclesiastical office did emerge early in the history of the Church. The first reference to deacons is in the epistle to the Philippians where Paul addressed himself to the "bishops and deacons" of the church at Philippi.[241] It is probable that the office of bishop emerged first, as the local leader of a diaspora church. As the churches grew larger, the bishops came to need the service of helpers, both in liturgical and in administrative functions. At some point such helpers came to be called "deacons," a title which formerly had designated all Christian ministers, but which gradually came to denote a specific office within the Church. During the time of Paul, when this transition in the meaning of the term was taking place, the word *diakonos* was used with both meanings, the general and the specific. By the end of the first century, in the pastoral epistles it is used only of the specific office of deacon.

A passage which may shed some light on this development is 1 Corinthians 16:15. Here Paul mentioned the household of Stephanas, who were the first converts in Asia. Since the time of their conversion, they had devoted themselves to the service *(diakonia)* of others. Paul urged the Christians of Corinth to recognize the legitimate authority of these persons. Many exegetes agree that *diakonia* in this passage designates at least an incipient form of church office.[242]

By the time of the pastoral epistles both the episcopacy and the diaconate were recognized as offices in the Church. 1 Timothy 3:8–13 lists the qualifications necessary for the office of deacon. This passage immediately follows the list of qualifications for the office of bishop. The deacons, like the bishops, were to be persons of good character, married only once and managing their own households well. There is an additional qualification for deacons, that they not be "double-tongued" or "slanderers." This may suggest that their ministry took them into people's homes, in closer and more intimate relationship with individual members of the Christian community.[243] Thus by the close of the New Testament period it is certain that the office of deacon existed at least within the pauline churches and that it was associated in subordinate relationship with the office of bishop.[244]

c. Charismatic Ministries. In his letters Paul wrote of the variety of the gifts of the Holy Spirit and of the diversity of ministries in the Church. He compared these to many members of one body, all working and suffering together. No one gift or ministry is sufficient by itself. What is important is that all be present, working together for the building up of the Christian community in faith and love.

In four different passages Paul gave lists of charismatic ministries which were exercised in the churches. The lists are not identical, although there is some basic overlapping.

1 Cor 12:8–10	1 Cor 12:28	Rm 12:7–8	Eph 4:11
wisdom	apostles	serving	apostles
knowledge	prophets	teaching	prophets
faith	teachers	exhorting	evangelists
healing	miracles	contributing	pastors
miracles	healers	giving aid	teachers
prophecy	helpers	acts of mercy	
discernment	administrators		
tongues	tongues		
interpretation	interpretation		

All of these lists are presented within the context of Paul's theology of the Church as the body of Christ. The ministries common to most of the lists are ministries of the word (apostle, prophet, teacher, evangelist), and ministries of service (serving, healing, helping, contributing, giving aid, acts of mercy and administration).

The charisms of ministry are, according to Paul, given to all Christians, irrespective of their office in the Church. All these charismatic ministries were found in the pauline churches, but not every charism was given to every Christian. The word "charism" became a technical term in pauline theology. Paul had a broad understanding of the meaning of the gifts of the Spirit and emphasized their diversity. The value of the charismata lay not in their possession, but in their exercise for the benefit of the community. The manifestation of the gifts was in no way due to any inherent talent or capacity of the person who received them. Rather they were given gratuitously by the Spirit for the service of the building up of the Christian community in love. The upbuilding of the Church through the exercise of the charismata contributes to its growth in unity as the body of Christ.[245] Each of the four passages listing the charismatic ministries culminates in an exhortation to love.[246] Love is both the principle of Christian unity and the greatest of the gifts of the Holy Spirit.

The ministry of the apostle has been discussed above. Suffice it to add here that in 1 Corinthians where apostleship is presented as a charismatic ministry, Paul described the functions of the apostle as preaching, correcting immorality and guiding the Church.[247] The ministry of the apostle is a gift of the Spirit which serves for the building up of the Church.

The second charismatic ministry is that of the prophet. It followed apostleship in importance in the churches. The Christian prophet was a proclaimer and interpreter of divine revelation. It is not certain how common the phenomenon of prophecy was in the early Church. Paul noted that not all Christians were prophets,[248] but that there were both men and women among the prophets.[249] Prophets were required to acknowledge the authority of Paul. At the same time there was some sort of ecclesiastical recognition of their status as prophets.[250]

In the pauline letters prophecy is described as serving the Christian community through edification, encouragement and consolation.[251] It is connected with knowledge and the understanding of mysteries.[252] Like the latter it is given only to those who are ruled by the Spirit.[253] Prophecy should be interpreted by the measure of faith and the prophet ought to prophesy only within the bounds of faith.[254] The prophet never stands for him/herself, but stands with other prophets who possess the same gift and authority within the Church. Through the Spirit (s)he is united with them and with the whole community. The authority of the prophet is not absolute.[255] It must be used for the building up of the Church and judged by the criterion of its confession of the lordship of Jesus.[256]

It is probable that the prophets were among the earliest presiders at the eucharistic liturgy. The *Didache*, which was composed around the end of the first century, concluded a lengthy treatise on the eucharist with a statement about the prophets as eucharistic celebrants.[257] Acts described prophets and teachers as ministering liturgically, using a verb which in the Septuagint was a technical term for cultic service.[258] The *Didache* used the same verb for the conduct of Christian worship both by prophets and teachers, and by bishops and deacons.[259] At this time liturgical leadership was beginning to pass to the bishops and deacons. However, the prophets and teachers at least in the community addressed were still more highly honored.[260] In the second century, prophecy as a special ministry disappeared as institution replaced charism and liturgical functions were subsumed by institutional offices.

Another prominent charismatic ministry was that of teaching. Already in the early letters of Paul teaching was an important mode of service in the Church. The function of teachers was to preserve, hand down and interpret the kerygma and to understand and explain the Hebrew scriptures. Paul himself had taught the Corinthians and handed down to them his own tradition or *halakah.*[261]

Prophecy and teaching were closely connected ministries. Both mediated the Spirit of Jesus and proclaimed his word. Both prophets and teachers presided at eucharistic worship. Both helped to build up the community. Both creatively transmitted the word of God to the Church. Both exercised some ministry of leadership in the Church. In Acts 13:1–2 it was the prophets and teachers of the church in Antioch who made the decision to choose Paul and Barnabas and send them forth on their first missionary journey. Paul and Barnabas were commissioned for their ministry through the imposition of hands by the prophets and teachers of Antioch.[262]

The administrators (*kuberneseis*) were those gifted by the Spirit to guide and direct the Christian community. This ministry was probably equivalent to that of presiding over the community (*proistamenos*).[263] Those who presided were exhorted to perform their ministry with zeal. It was they who governed the community in the Lord.[264] The epistle to the Hebrews mentioned "leaders" (*hegoumenoi*) who exercised authority and a ministry of word and care in the community.[265]

Administrators seem not to have been the most important ministers in the community. Apostles, prophets and teachers were always mentioned first. The forms and titles of administrative office in the earliest decades of church history were quite diverse. Administrators did hold and exercise authority in the early Church, but it was an authority of service, and less than the authority of the primary ministers of the word.

It is not justified on the basis of the New Testament evidence to set the charismatic ministries in contradistinction to the official ministries, such as those of apostle and deacon, presbyter and bishop.[266] There is much overlapping. One office, that of apostle, is also listed by Paul among the charismatic ministries. It is possible that the offices of presbyter and bishop grew out of the earlier charismatic ministries of administration. The holders of many early church offices frequently exercised the charismatic ministries of teaching, preaching, exhorting, healing, helping and serving. Charism and office were complementary dimensions of Christian ministry. Charismata without some sort of official structuring often led to conflict or chaos within the community. And office without the charismata could become sterile and fossilized.

The charismatic ministries gradually disappeared from the life of the Church after the first century as they were absorbed into the offices of bishop, priest and deacon. The institution of ecclesiastical office came to replace the phenomenon of charismatic ministry. Yet as the Holy Spirit was always present and active in the Church, offering gifts to all Christians, various forms of charismatic ministry re-emerged in various times and places in history, and not always within the official institutions. Insofar as Christian ministry is grounded in the gifts of the Holy Spirit, the charismatic dimension of ministry should remain an integral and important aspect of ecclesiastical office.

Administrative Office in the Early Church

a. The Structures of Administrative Office. Administration first emerged as a charismatic ministry of service. At the time when it first appears in the letters to the churches of Corinth and Rome, the primary authority was still that of the missionary apostle Paul. In the following decade the missionary apostles began to die off, leaving a vacuum of authority in which it soon became necessary for some sort of local leadership to emerge. Local officials began to appear in the rapidly growing churches of the empire. In some locales they were called "presbyters" or "elders," and in others "bishops" or "overseers."

The traditional understanding of this development has been that the office of presbyter grew out of the tradition of synagogue elders in the Jewish Christian communities. The office of bishop developed in the gentile churches with some connection to the secular Greek office of overseer. However, the actual historical development was far more complex. What may prove to be a more correct understanding of the process is the following. After both Jewish and gentile churches had been founded by missionary apostles, these apostles eventually died or went elsewhere. As the communities grew larger some form of structure became necessary. Local leaders emerged and, after the disappearance of the founding apostles, came to exercise sole authority over their churches. In the communities whose background lay in the pharisaic, rabbinic Judaism of the synagogue, the structure and terminology of the presbyterate were used. In the churches with some contact with sectarian Essene Judaism or possibly also with Greek structures, the term "bishop" was used.[267]

Acts 20 indicates that in at least some churches the two titles, presbyter and bishop, were interchangeable.[268] In Luke's introduction to the passage the officials were called presbyters of Ephesus. But within Paul's speech to them, they were addressed as bishops. Another indication that this was the situation is a variant reading of 1 Peter 5:2 in which the presbyters are exhorted to exercise the function of "overseeing" (*episkopein*). The two titles are used in parallel and probably synonymously also in Titus.[269]

Thus it is possible that the two offices, originating independently soon merged into one, possibly as early as during the lifetime of Paul. The office of presbyter may have originated first, but then been modified through the influence of the Essene office of overseer. The office of presbyter-bishop developed early and appeared in both Jewish and gentile Christian communities. Those who held this office were not in any historically verifiable way successors of the Twelve. They did take over the leadership role of the missionary apostles, although there is no evidence that they were directly commissioned by the apostles to do so. But that leadership role was modified insofar as they were resident rather than itinerant leaders.[270]

b. Bishop. The Greek word *"episkopos"* means "overseer." It was used in Greek both of gods and of men, some of whom were state or local officials. In the Septuagint the word is used in the same two ways. It does not denote any sort of religious function, although there were overseers in charge of the financial affairs of Greek cults.[271] However, the Christian office is probably not rooted in the Greek usage of the term.

The Essene office of overseer has closer parallels. The Greek word *"episkopos"* is an exact translation of the Hebrew words *"pāqid"* and *"mᵉbaqqēr,"* both of which denoted an administrative official in the Essene community of Qumran. This official was responsible for community property, for choosing and instructing novices seeking membership in the community, and for judging the conduct of the members. In the literature of Qumran this office was connected with the symbolic image of the shepherd tending his flock.[272] Josephus used the same Greek verb for the appointment of overseers among the Essenes which the *Didache* used for the Christian appointment of bishops.[273]

In the New Testament the first epistle of Peter called Jesus himself *episkopos.*[274] In the context of the verse the overseeing of souls is set parallel to the image of the shepherding of a flock. This same image of shepherd is found in conjunction with the exhortation to presbyter-bishops in Acts 20:28. This passage continues, enjoining the bishops to guard against false teachers in their community.

In the pastoral epistles 1 Timothy 3 lists the qualifications for bishops: good character, teaching ability and a good marriage with well-behaved children. The pastorals demonstrate that at the end of the first century bishops were expected to function as stewards of community property, holding firm to tradition, instructing the community in sound doctrine, and refuting those who taught falsely.[275]

c. **Presbyter.** The Greek word *presbyteros* denotes an older person, an elder. Despite the English derivative, it does not mean "priest." In Judaism at the time of Jesus, every synagogue was governed by a council of elders called the *gerousia* in Greek. Besides administration, another important function of the Jewish elders was the preservation and interpretation of religious tradition. Officials of various Greek religions and also secular officials such as the leader of a village were also called "elders" in the contemporary Mediterranean world. The Christian institution of the elder, however, derived primarily from the synagogue office.

In the church of Jerusalem there were elders who were associated with the apostles as the ruling authorities of the church.[276] It was these elders who received the collection of aid sent by the church of Antioch.[277] They were consulted on religious questions and participated with the apostles in official decisions.[278] James and the elders received the report of the returning missionary Paul.[279]

There were also elders in the churches of the diaspora.[280] Some of these had been appointed by Paul and Barnabas.[281] The pastoral functions of such elders were anointing and praying over the sick, and taking care of the flock through the generosity and humility of their example.[282]

In the pastoral epistles the appointment of elders was further delegated from Paul to Titus.[283] This passage, which lists the qualifications for the office of presbyter-bishop, is ambiguous as to whether one or two distinct offices are being described. It is probable that at this time what had originally been two distinct offices were in the process of merging into one.

Elders are described in 1 Timothy 5:17 as ruling the churches, preaching and teaching. According to Titus 1:9 these are functions of the bishop. 1 Timothy 4:14 mentions a college of elders (*presbyterion*) which years earlier had laid hands upon Timothy conferring on him the gifts of the Spirit.

Thus in different areas and in communities of different backgrounds local church leadership developed through somewhat different forms and titles. But as time went on, with the excellent communications system of the Roman empire, both the form and title of the office of church leader became increasingly standardized. The offices of bishop and presbyter merged into one and retained the title of bishop. Then as the churches grew even larger, when the bishop was no longer able to manage all the affairs and preside over all the worship of his diocese by himself, some of his functions were delegated to lower clergy, to deacons in the first century, and to other officials who took the title, but not the mode of office, of presbyters in the second century.

Conclusion

In the Old Testament there were two major traditions of ministry: priesthood and ministry of the word. The first tradition is not found in the New Testament as a model for Christian ministry. The connotations of priesthood in the Old Testament of power and status are antithetical to the nature of Christian ministry in the new covenant. Most of the official ministries in the New Testament derive from or are similar to offices in the Old Testament tradition of the word: disciple, apostle, prophet, teacher, elder.

The ministry of Jesus was similar to that of the rabbi. But there were essential differences. More important than teaching was his ministry of suffering service, of total self-offering on the cross. When Jesus taught his disciples about the nature of ministry he expected of them, he qualified the rabbinic model of disciple with the Isaian theology of the suffering servant. Jesus' own ministry of priesthood finally resembled the priestly self-offering of the suffering servant more closely than it did the animal sacrifices of the levitical priests.

The basic core of Christian tradition on the meaning of ministry, upon which an authentic theology of ministry must build, is found in the words and actions of Jesus. Jesus himself ultimately ministered as servant and he taught his disciples to minister as servants.

The Jewish traditions of priesthood and synagogue office were inherently sexist institutions, priesthood by law and synagogue office by custom. The ministry of servant was new and unique and had not been connected with any formal religious office in the history of Judaism. There was a greater freedom for the inclusion of all human persons in the new ministerial model of servanthood. As long as servant remained the primary model for Christian ministry women were able to minister on the same basis as men. When, at the close of the New Testament period the Christian model of servant was replaced by Jewish models of presbyter and bishop, and in the second century the Old Testament model of levitical priesthood was applied to ecclesiastical office, women came to be excluded from the official ministry of the Church.

NOTES

1. In the prehistorical period, Cain and Abel were said to have made offerings (Gn 4:3–5) and Noah to have built an altar and made burnt offerings (Gn 8:20). There are many aetiological stories in Genesis which explain the origin of a sanctuary or holy place by connecting it to a story about a patriarchal figure. Abraham is described as building altars at Shechem (Gn 12:7) and Hebron (Gn 13:8). He prepared to offer his own son, Isaac, in sacrifice on Mt. Moriah (Gn 22: 2–3). Isaac is reputed to have built an altar at Beersheba (Gn 26:25). Likewise Jacob also built an altar at Shechem (Gn 33:20) and one at Bethel (37:7) where he founded a sanctuary by setting up a pillar and pouring oil over it (28:18–22). There he made a drink offering (35:14). Jacob also offered sacrifice at Mizpah where his kinsmen shared in the eating of the bread (31:54). Near the end of his life, Jacob, now called Israel, offered sacrifices at Beersheba in thanksgiving that his son, Joseph, was still alive (46:1).
2. Levi is mentioned in the list of the twelve sons of Jacob in Gn 29:31–30:24, 35:23–26, Ex 1:1–5, Dt 27:12–13, Ezek 48:31–34, 1 Chr 2:1–2, and in the blessings of the twelve tribes of Israel in Gn 49:3–27 and Dt 33:6–29. Other later lists omit Levi and replace Joseph with Ephraim and Manasseh, reflecting the situation in the land after the settlement: Nm 1:5–15, 20–43, 2:3–31, 7:12–83, 13:4–15, 26:5–50, Jos 13–19. Cf. Nm 1:47–50.
3. The Blessings of Moses (Dt 33:8–11) attribute priestly functions to the tribe of Levi, reflecting the situation in the early years of the monarchy when this text was composed. In the Blessings of Jacob (Gn 49:5–7), which date from the eleventh century B.C. or earlier, Simeon and Levi, both secular tribes, were judged and dispersed.
4. Ex 19:22, 24.
5. Ex 2:1. Ex 4:14 confirms the levitical ancestry of Moses' brother, Aaron, also. This is confirmed again in Ex 6:16–20 and Nm 26:59 (P).
6. Ex 29:20–21 (P), Lv 8:23–24 (P).
7. Aelred Cody, *A History of Old Testament Priesthood, Analecta Biblica* 35 (Rome: Pontifical Biblical Institute, 1969), p. 59.
8. *Ibid.*, pp. 26–29, 60–61.
9. In Ugarit and Phoenicia, the *khnm* were urban priests. The resemblance between these and the Israelite *kohanim* increased after the settlement and during the monarchy as Israelite culture became increasingly urban.

10. Jdg 17–18, 1 Sm 1–4, 22:9–23.

11. 1 Kg 1:5–8, 44, 2:26–27. Cf. Cody, *op. cit.*, pp. 91–92. It is possible that Abiathar supported Adonijah because of his pure Israelite ancestry, whereas Zadok, himself a Jebusite, supported Solomon whose mother may herself also have been Jebusite (cf. 2 Sm 5:13–14).

12. The Jebusites were a Canaanite tribe, located in the area of the city-state of Salem or Jerusalem.

13. H. H. Rowley, "Melchizedek and Zadok (Gen 14 and Ps 110)," *Festschrift Alfred Bertholet zum 80. Geburtstag* (Tübingen: Mohr, 1950), pp. 461–472, "Zadok and Nehustan," *Journal of Biblical Literature* 58 (1939), pp. 113–141. Against this view cf. Roland De Vaux, *Ancient Israel* (New York: McGraw-Hill, 1961), II, p. 374, and Paul D. Hanson, *The Dawn of Apocalyptic* (Philadelphia: Fortress, 1975), p. 221.

14. The first, Gn 14:18–20, was an aetiological story attributed to ancient times (and possibly based upon an ancient Abraham legend) in which Abram, by offering tithes to Melchizedek, recognized and legitimated the priesthood of the latter. Rowley also associates Ps 110 with the time of David, and specifically with the ceremony of his institution as ruler of Jerusalem. David's policy toward the Jebusites was generally tolerant and merciful, even to the extent of recognizing the priesthood of the current Jebusite high priest. There are parallels in this psalm to ancient Canaanite fertility rites. The form of the psalm is a dialogical liturgy. In the first and last three verses, Zadok, according to Rowley, is addressing King David, confirming him as ruler of Jerusalem. In verse 4 (to and from which there is an awkward transition) David addressed Zadok, confirming him as priest of Jerusalem, by mentioning the most ancient known priest of Jerusalem, Melchizedek, and by pronouncing the name of his Lord, thus making the confirmation of Zadok's priesthood solemnly irrevocable. Cf. Rowley, "Melchizedek," pp. 466–470. Much of Rowley's theory would be plausible even if the psalm had been composed later, perhaps during the reign of Solomon, for the purpose of legitimizing the priesthood of Zadok, who by that time was the sole head of the Israelite cult.

15. The term "great" or "high" priest is mentioned only four times in pre-exilic texts (2 Kg 12:10, 22:4, 8, 23:4). The office and terminology of high priesthood were not yet as precisely defined as they came to be after the exile.

16. 2 Kg 25:18 = Jer 52:24. Cf. 2 Kg 22:4.

17. 1 Sm 2:22, Ex 38:8 (P).

18. Hanson, *op. cit.*, p. 212.

19. Cf. Jer 41:4–5.

20. Ezekiel made an explicit distinction between levites and priests (Ezek 44:9–31). Levites were to serve the Temple, but were not to be allowed to approach the sanctuary (44:11–14). Zadokite priests would serve in the sanctuary in the presence of God (44:15). Kings (and even their corpses) were not permitted henceforth in the sanctuary at all (43:7–8).

21. Nm 18:6–7.

22. Nm 18:6. Cf. Nm 16:1–11, 40: the story of Korah was told to warn non-aaronite levites not to attempt to perform the functions of priests.

23. The Pharisees protested the assumption of the high priestly office by Jonathan. Later Alexander Jannaeus put eight hundred Pharisees to death for their opposition. Even stronger was the opposition of the Essenes. This sect went into exile in the Judean wilderness at Qumran in protest over the illegitimacy of the Jerusalem priesthood.

24. Between 37 B.C. and A.D. 67 there were 28 high priests, 25 of whom were from non-legitimate priestly families. In 67 A.D. the Zealots chose a new zadokite high priest by lot. Cf. Josephus, *War* IV, 147–148.

25. Walther Eichrodt, *Theology of the Old Testament* (Philadelphia: Westminster, 1961), I, pp. 406, 410.

26. Jdg 17:10, 12, 18:4, 1 Kg 13:33.

27. Nm 8:10.

28. Nm 27:15–23. The P editor notes the presence of the priest Eleazar, but Moses is the subject of the verbs and therefore the one who imposed hands.

29. Ex 29:4–7, 40:12–15, Lv 8:6–12; Zech 3:1–9 lacks the third stage.

30. Ex 28:41, 30:30, 40:12-15, Lv 7:35–36, Nm 3:3. These references were inserted into the earlier narratives by later P editors.

31. The eighth through the sixth centuries B.C., beginning with Amos and continuing through Malachi after the exile.

32. Johannes Pedersen, *Israel. Its Life and Culture* (London: Oxford University Press, 1940), III–IV, p. 159.

33. Miriam in Ex 15:20 (cf. Mic 6:3–4 and Nm 12), Deborah in Jdg 4:4, Huldah in 2 Kg 22:14–20, the wife of Isaiah in Is 8:3, and Noadiah in Neh 6:14.

34. Joel 2:28.

35. The wise woman of Tekoa is described in 2 Sm 14:2–20, the wise woman of Abel in 2 Sm 20:15–22, the wise women of the court of Sisera in Jdg 5:29.

36. Ber 33a.

37. George F. Moore, *Judaism in the First Centuries of the Christian Era* (Cambridge: Harvard University Press, 1927), I, p. 284.

38. Egypt, Moab, Midian, Greece and Rome.

39. Jdg 8:14.

40. Dt 21:18–21, 1 Sm 30:26–31.

41. 2 Sm 5:3. Cf. 1 Sm 8:4, 2 Sm 3:17, 17:4, 1 Kg 12:6, 21:8–13, 2 Kg 10:5, 23:1.

42. Ezek 8:1, 14:1, 20:1, 3.

43. Ezr 5:5, 9, 6:7, 14, 10:8, 14.

44. 1 Mc 7:33, 12:35, 13:36, Jud 6:21, 7:23, 10:6.

45. Dt 21:19–21, 22:15–18, 25:7–9, Prv 31:23. Cf. Gn 23:10, 18, Jb 29:7, Prv 24:7.

46. 1 Kg 21:8–12, 2 Kg 10:1–11.

47. Dt 21:1–9. Cf. Dt 19:11–13.

48. Ex 3:16–18, 4:29, 17:5, 24:1–2, 9–11 (J).

49. De Vaux, *op. cit.,* II, p. 347, states that in postbiblical Judaism, imposition of hands was used only for the installation or ordination of rabbis. The rabbis considered themselves the heirs of the elders of the Old Testament. The rationale for the practice of laying on of hands was found in the rabbinic interpretation of Nm 11:16–17: since Moses had laid hands upon Joshua in Nm 27:15–23, then he must have done the same when giving the spirit to the seventy elders in Nm 11:16–17.

50. *Rosh hakknesset* in Hebrew, *archisynagogos* in Greek.

51. Massey H. Shepherd, "Elder in the New Testament," *Interpreter's Dictionary of the Bible* (New York: Abingdon, 1962), II, p. 73.

52. Mk 7:3–5, Mt 15:2.

53. Moore, *op. cit.,* pp. 289–290. It was not permitted for the *hazzan* to be a priest. Cf. Lk 4:20.

54. Meg 23a.

55. Oepke, *TDNT* I, p. 782.

56. Jer 33:14–26, Zech 4:14, Mal 3:1–5, 23–24, Test Reub 6:6–12, Test Sim 7:1–2, Test Lev 18:2–14, Test Dan 5:10–13, 1QSa 2:12–14, 19, 1QS 9:11, CD 12:23, 14:19, 19:10, 20:1.

57. Is 42:1–4, 49:1–6, 50:4–9, 52:13, 53:12.

58. Jesus was addressed in Aramaic as *rabbi* or *rabboni.* These terms were often translated into Greek in the NT as *didaskalos* ("teacher").

59. Mt 4:23, 9:35, 13:54, Mk 1:21, 6:2, Lk 4:15, 31–33, 6:6, Jn 18:20.

60. Mk 12:35, 14:49 pars., Lk 19:47, 21:37–38, Jn 7:14, 8:20, 18:20. It is possible that Jesus taught in the synagogue which was located within the precincts of the Second Temple, rather than in the Temple itself.

61. Mk 12:14 pars.

62. Mt 5:21–26, 27–30, 33–37. The teaching of Jesus was handed down in much the same form as that of other contemporary rabbis: short aphorisms, which were often set within the framework of a dialogue. Cf. C. H. Dodd, "Jesus as Teacher and Prophet," in G. K. Bell and A. Deissmann, *Mysterium Christi* (London: Longman, Green, 1930), p. 53. Jesus was asked to give his own summary of the law (Mk 12:28–34 pars) which he reduced to the commandment to love God and other persons (as did Hillel, cf. Dodd, *art. cit.,* p. 55). Jesus was also asked his opinion on theological questions and current religious issues, as for example the Sadducean objection to belief in resurrection (Mk 12:18–29 pars) or the number of persons who would be saved (Lk 13:23–24) or the davidic ancestry of the messiah (Mk 12:35–37 pars).

63. For example in the Sermon on the Mount in Mt 5–7 and in some of the apocalyptic sayings in Mk 13.

64. Mk 1:22, 11:18, Mt 7:29.

65. Jesus reversed current interpretations of scripture on questions

such as oaths and divorce. He seems to have contradicted the literal meaning
of the Torah on the question of defilement in Mk 7:15 par. Cf. Dodd, *art.
cit.,* p. 56.

66. Lk 5:17, 6:6, 13:10–11. In Jn 9, in the story of the man born blind,
teaching is connected with healing, and healing with bearing witness to Jesus.

67. Mk 4:38, 5:35, 9:17, 10:51 pars., Jn 3:2.

68. Mk 9:1 pars.

69. Mk 4:11 pars.

70. Mk 9:43 pars., 10:26 pars.

71. Jn 7:16.

72. Jn 8:28. The Holy Spirit will also teach the followers of Jesus and
help them understand what Jesus had taught them (Jn 14:26). The Spirit
would also teach them through his anointing (1 Jn 2:27).

73. Cf. Prv 8:4–17, 9:5–6, Sir 1:16, 24:19–22. In the fourth gospel, Jesus himself was presented as personified wisdom. He, like wisdom, was pre-
existent and had a role in God's creation of the world. Jesus' place, like that
of wisdom, is with God, yet he dwells among men and women. He proceeded from God's glory and light. And he is for human persons a source of life.
He is descended from on high whence human beings cannot rise by themselves. He reveals heavenly things. He also, like wisdom, delivers men and
women from darkness and death. He instructs disciples who become his children, as wisdom also instructed her children.

74. The synoptic portrait of Jesus does not explicitly proclaim, but
also does not exclude, the possibility of his priesthood. The Lukan infancy
narrative notes that Elizabeth had aaronite ancestry and that Mary was her
relative (Lk 1:5, 36). Jesus' baptism (Mk 1:10–11 pars.) has been understood
as a solemn investiture into priesthood, on the basis of Test Lev 18:2ff. '(cf.
Jean Colson, *Ministère de Jésus-Christ ou le sacerdoce de l'Évangile* (Paris:
Beauchesne, 1966), p. 87). The stronger image in the baptismal scene, however, was that of the suffering servant. During the course of his ministry, Jesus is portrayed both as being loyal to the existing institution of the Jewish
priesthood (Mk 1:44, Mt 8:4, Lk 5:14, 17:14) and also as challenging its priv-
ileged status (Mk 2:26–28 pars, Lk 10:31–37). Jesus purged the Temple of
contemporary corrupt practices (Mk 11:15–17 pars.). In Mt 12:6 Jesus is
presented as revealing himself as greater than the Temple and its cult and
even than the Torah itself. It is possible that the predictions of Jesus' destruction and replacement of the Temple (Mk 14:58 pars., Jn 2:19–21) are
rooted in actual sayings of Jesus, as opposed to later statements (Mt 9:13,
12:7, Ac 6:13–14, 7:48) which reflect a theological polemic against the Temple. The synoptic gospels present Jesus as performing the priestly function of
blessing (Lk 24:50–51). Several passages connect a saying of Jesus with Ps
110, which the Epistle to the Hebrews connected with the priesthood of Jesus (Mk 12:35–37 pars., 14:62 pars.). Jesus is presented in white vestments,
like those of a priest, in the transfiguration accounts (Mk 9:3 pars). Jesus is

addressed by the priestly title "holy one of God" in Mk 1:24 par., Jn 6:69 (cf Lv 21:6, 2 Chr 23:6, 35:3). The idea that Jesus established a new covenant, which was a semi-priestly act connected with the suffering servant, is suggested in the synoptic gospels (Lk 22:20). In the last supper accounts, Jesus is portrayed as offering his life as a ransom for many in sacrificial cultic language which also recalls the suffering servant (Mk 10:45 pars., 14:22–25 pars.). Thus the synoptic portrayal of Jesus as priest frequently is qualified by the model of the suffering servant, and nowhere explicitly linked with the model of levitical priesthood.

75. Priestly connotations are not completely absent from the christology of the pauline epistles. Jesus, the risen and exalted Christ, makes intercession for the followers (Rm 8:34). God's redemptive act through Jesus accomplished what the cultic practices of the Torah could not (Rm 8:3). Jesus established a new covenant through his death and resurrection (1 Cor 11:25, 2 Cor 3:6). This was a function of the servant of II Isaiah. Some scholars have concluded that the establishment of a new covenant meant de facto the establishment of a new priesthood (and a priesthood which was new in precisely the same manner as the new covenant). Cf. Oscar Cullmann, *The Christology of the New Testament* (Philadelphia: Westminster, 1959), p. 104; André Feuillet, *The Priesthood of Christ and His Ministers* (Garden City: Doubleday, 1975), p. 11. Jesus, like the high priest of the old covenant, and through him the people, have access to the presence of God (Rm 5:2, Eph 2:18). Jesus, like the suffering servant, was killed for the sins of others (Rm 3:25, 4:25). His death and resurrection were a sacrifice such as that of passover (1 Cor 5:7) or Yom Kippur (Rm 3:25). Christ's sacrifice was not merely the offering of a victim, but the offering of himself in a supreme act of love (Eph 5:2). In this sense, though, he resembled the suffering servant more than the levitical priests.

76. In the fourth gospel, priesthood and sacrifice are spiritualized in much the same way as they are in the fourth servant song in Is 52–53 (cf. Colson, *op. cit.,* p. 88; Feuillet, *op. cit.,* p. 81). According to Feuillet (*op. cit.,* pp. 32–33) the figures of the suffering servant and the eschatological priest are inseparably connected. The servant is himself a priest. The two concepts are explicitly linked in the proclamation of Jesus as the "lamb of God" (servant and paschal victim) in Jn 1:29, 36. In Jn Jesus is even more explicitly proclaimed as replacing the Temple by himself (2:19–21). This saying is set at the time of passover (2:13, 23). Elsewhere Jesus is portrayed as offering himself as the paschal victim (6:4, 51–58). Like the lamb of passover (Ex 12:46), when Jesus is killed, no bone of his body is broken (Jn 19:36). The blood of Jesus' sacrifice will purify his followers from their sins (1 Jn 1:7). Jesus is portrayed as laying down his life, like the servant, as a sacrifice, for the people (Jn 10:11, 15, 17) (Colson, *op. cit.,* p. 94 understands Jn 10:8 as a pejorative reference to the Jewish priesthood). Jesus is presented explicitly as sacrifice in 1 Jn 2:2, 4:10 (*hilasmos,* "expiation") and as present intercessor

and mediator in 1 Jn 2:1. In the johannine passion narrative, Jesus is portrayed as dressed in garments which reflect the vestments of the high priest
(Jn 19:23–24) which are without seam (Ex 28:32) and which are not to be
torn (Lv 21:10). In Rev 1:13 the glorified Christ is revealed as the Son of
Man in similar high priestly vestments (the term *poeres* appears in the LXX
of Ex 28:4, 29:5). The prayer of Jesus in Jn 17 has often been called his "high
priestly prayer." Prayer itself (17:9, 15, 20) is often, though not exclusively,
a priestly function. Feuillet understands this chapter in reference to the high
priestly sacrifice of Yom Kippur, both in structure and in content (*op. cit.,*
pp. 51–71). His thesis is not impossible, but the paucity of concrete evidence
in its support has contributed to its lack of acceptance among other scholars.

77. Hb 13:22.
78. Hb 3:5–6.
79. Hb 4:14–5:10.
80. Ps 110:4. The levitical priests did not hold an eternal priesthood
because they died. Hb 7 legitimated the priesthood of Jesus by reference to
the story of Melchizedek in Gn 14:18–20 and the allusion to his priesthood
in Ps 110:4. The argument is that Abraham, who contained within himself
the seed of Levi and of all Levi's descendents, paid tithes to the priest-king
Melchizedek, thus recognizing the legitimacy of his priesthood. Levi and
Aaron, because they were inside Abraham, also paid homage to Melchizedek. Melchizedek accepted the tithes and blessed Abraham (and his seed). It
is possible that this argument reflected some sympathy to the house of Zadok (who were disenfranchised from the Temple priesthood in the first century) on the part of the Jewish-Christian readers of the epistle. Christians
coming from a background in Essene Judaism might have had such a problem (cf. 1QapGn, 11QMelch).

81. Hb 8:1–6.
82. Hb 9.
83. Hb 10:1–18.
84 Is 49:6.
85. Is 53:5–8.
86. Hb 9:15, 12:17, 28, 13:1.
87. Hb 13:9, 15–16.
88. Hb 12:12–16, 13:1–3.
89. Ex 4:10, Nm 11:11, Dt 3:24.
90. Is 56:6.
91. Is 49:5–6.
92. J. Jeremias, "Pais theou," *TDNT* V, p. 666.
93. Ben Sira, Ethiopian Enoch, Peshitta, Tg Is 42:1, 43:10, 52:13.
94. Is 49:5. Is 42:1 (chosen), 49:1 (called and named), 42:1 (endowed
with spirit).
95. Is 53:1–12.
96. Is 42:1, 3–4 (*mishpat*).

97. Is 49:6.
98. Is 53:5–12 (suffering), 49:4 (cf. 49:7), 50:7–9, 52:15, 53:12 (vindication).
99. Ezek 34:23–24, 37:24–25, Zech 3:8, 4 Ezr 7:28, 13:32, 37, 52, Syr Bar 70:9, and also targums on these passages.
100. Except Test Ben 3:8, which may be post-Christian. Cf. Cullmann, *op. cit.*, p. 56.
101. Mt 12:18, Ac 3:13, 26, 4:27, 30.
102. Mt 8:17 (Is 53:4), 12:17–21 (Is 42:1–4), Lk 22:37 (Is 53:12), Jn 12:38 (Is 53:1), Ac 8:32–33 (Is 53:7–8), Rm 15:21 (Is 52:15).
103. 1 Cor 11:23–25, 15:3–5, Rm 4:25, 8:34, Phl 2:6–11, Gal 1:4, Eph 5:2, 25, 1 Tm 2:6, Tit 2:14.
104. Mk 1:10–11 pars., 9:12 pars., 10:45 pars., 14:24 pars., Mt 20:28, and the passion predictions in Mk 8:31, 9:31, 10:33.
105. Jn 1:29, 34, 36, 3:14, 12:34, 1 Jn 2:2, 3:5, 7, 4:10.
106. Is 42:1.
107. Mt 11:2–6, Is 35:5–6, 61:1.
108. Cullmann, *op. cit.,* p. 65.
109. Jn 1:29–36. Cullmann, *op. cit.*, p. 71 (cites Burney and Jeremias).
110. Ac 8:26–40, Is 53:7–8.
111. Mk 9:12 pars., 10:45 pars., Mt 20:28, Lk 22:27.
112. Mk 10:43–44 pars.
113. Mk 10:43 (RSV).
114. The servant was given the title of "priest" in Philo, *De spec. leg.* I, 116.
115. Mt 4:9–10 par., Mk 10:43–45.
116. Mt 8:16–17 (Is 53:4), Mk 10:45.
117. Mk 10:44.
118. Mt 6:5–6.
119. Mk 1:21–22, 39, 3:1, 6:2 pars., Mt 9:35, Lk 4:15–16, 13:10.
120. Lk 5:16, 6:12.
121. In Lk there are nine references to Jesus' private prayer, seven of which occur in passages based on L.
122. Before the descent of the Spirit in Lk 3:21, after the call of the disciples and the first healings in 5:16, before the choosing of the Twelve in 6:12, before Peter's confession and the prediction of the passion in 9:18, at the transfiguration in 9:28–29, before the teaching on the Lord's prayer in 11:1, at Gethsemane in 22:41–45, and on the cross in 23:34, 46.
123. Mk 14:35, 36, Lk 22:41–45, Hb 5:7, Jn 12:27. According to J. Jeremias, *The Prayers of Jesus* (London: S.C.M., 1967), pp. 11–65, prayers which contain the Aramaic word *"Abba"* ("father") are early and most probably actual sayings of Jesus. The problem of the disciples being asleep and therefore unable to witness Jesus' prayer is not insurmountable. The primary saying is Jesus' command to "watch." The statement about the dis-

ciples being asleep may have been added secondarily in response to this and thus not be historical.

124. Mk 15:34, Mt 27:46, Lk 23:34, 46.

125. Mk, Q, M and L.

126. Mk 11:24 par., Lk 11:5–13, 18:1–8.

127. Mt 18:19–20.

128. Mt 6:6–13, Lk 11:2–4.

129. Mk 1:9–11 pars.

130. James D. Dunn, *Jesus and the Spirit* (Philadelphia: Westminster, 1975), pp. 44–53, cites relevant passages.

131. It began with Socrates and the Academy of Plato and continued through the later schools such as the Pythagorean. It was also operative in the mystery religions. Cf. K. H. Rengstorf, *"mathetes,"* *TDNT* IV, pp. 419–426.

132. Rengstorf, *TDNT* IV, 427.

133. Is 50:4, 54:13, Jer 31:33–34.

134. Sir 38:25, 39:11. Cf. Rengstorf, *TDNT* IV, p. 435.

135. Jn 9:28.

136. Ac 22:3.

137. Mk 1:17–20 pars., Jn 1:38–50.

138. Jn 6:39, 10:29, 17:6, 12.

139. Mt 8:19, Lk 9:57.

140. Mk 8:34–35 pars., 10:21 pars., Mt 8:19.

141. Mt 6:24 par., 8:19–22 par., 10:37–39 par.

142. Jn 8:13–15, 31.

143. Mk 8:34, 10:38, Mt 19:28–29, Lk 22:28.

144. Rengstorf, *TDNT* IV, p. 455.

145. Mt 10:37, Lk 14:26.

146. Mk 10:17–31 pars.

147. Mk 8:34–38 pars.

148. Mk 9:33–36 pars., 10:42–44 pars.

149. Mt 13:16–17, Lk 10:23–24.

150. Mk 13:9–13 pars.

151. Mt 10:7 par., Mk 16:15.

152. Mt 28:20.

153. Lk 24:48.

154. Mt 28:19.

155. Mt 10:8, Lk 9:1, 6, Mk 6:13.

156. Mk 6:7 pars., 9:28 par., Mt 10:1, 8, Lk 10:17–20.

157. Lk 17:3–4, Mt 18:21–22.

158. Mk 2:1–12 pars.

159. Mk 8:1–10 par.

160. Mk 6:37.

161. Jn 6. Raymond E. Brown, *The Gospel According to John, Anchor*

Bible 29 (Garden City: Doubleday, 1966, 1970), I, p. 274, discusses the "possible eucharistic undertones" in the passage.

162. Mk 10:35–45 pars. Cf. Mk 9:33–37 pars.

163. Mt 23:8–12 (RSV).

164. Mk 3:13–19, Lk 6:12–16, Mt 10:1–4.

165. Mk 6:7–13, Mt 10:1, 5–23, Lk 9:1–6.

166. Lk 10:1–20. Cf. Mt 9:37–38.

167. Lk 10:9.

168. Lk 10:16. Cf. Mt 10:40, where this is applied to the Twelve.

169. Mk 3:7–8, Mt 4:25, Lk 6:17, 14:25.

170. Jn 1:38–40 (Nathanael), 3:1–21 (Nicodemus), Mk 15:43 pars. (Joseph of Arimathea).

171. Lk 8:1–3.

172. *Shaliah* is the Aramaic equivalent of the Greek word *apostolos*.

173. Hb 3:1.

174. Ac 4:5–22, 5:27–42.

175. Mk 16:15, Mt 28:19–20, Lk 24:47–48, Jn 20:21, Ac 1:8.

176 The few references to the word "apostle" in the gospels were retrojected into the lifetime of Jesus by the evangelists who were writing much later.

177. 1 Cor 9:1–2, 15:3–9.

178. Ac 1:21–22.

179. Jn 20:21–23.

180. The lists of names of the Twelve are found in Mk 3:16–19, Mt 10:2–4, Lk 6:14–16, Ac 1:13. The existence of the Twelve is mentioned in Jn 6:67, 20:24.

181. Mk 3:14–15 pars.

182. Mk 6:30, Mt 10:2, Lk 6:13, 9:10, 17:5, 22:14, 24:10 are anachronistic in their use of the term. The word was used most often in the gospel of Lk, for whom it was a substitute for the "twelve."

183. Lk 11:49 par., Mt 23:34.

184. K. Rengstorf, *"Dodeka,"* *TDNT* II, pp. 324–328.

185. Elisabeth S. Fiorenza, "The Role of Women According to Luke/ Acts," unpublished address to the General Meeting of the Catholic Biblical Association of America, San Francisco, August 24, 1978, E. S. Fiorenza, "The Twelve," in Swidler, *Women Priests,* pp. 114–122.

186. Ac 1:13–14. E. S. Fiorenza, "The Apostleship of Women in Early Christianity," in Swidler, *Women Priests,* pp. 135–136.

187. Mary of Magdala was the most prominent leader of the early Church according to the gnostic Gospel According to Mary. Cf. Raymond E. Brown, "Roles of Women in the Fourth Gospel," *Theological Studies* 36 (1975), p. 693.

188. Both Peter and the apostles in general seem to have exercised leadership and made decisions collegially. Cf. Ac 8:14, 11:1–18, 15:6–11.

189. Gal 1:18.

190. This may have been the case in Ac 6. There was a contemporary example of an administrative body of twelve at Qumran. Cf. 1QS 8:1. However this consisted of twelve men and three priests. John L. McKenzie, *Authority in the Church* (New York: Sheed & Ward, 1966), p. 49, considers that the only administrative act as such in the early Jerusalem church was that of community property. Cf. Ac 4:32–35.

191. Ac 12:2.

192. C. 40 A.D. Cf. Joseph A. Fitzmyer, "A Life of Paul," *The Jerome Biblical Commentary* (Englewood Cliffs, New Jersey: Prentice-Hall, 1968), II, p. 218. Cf. Gal 1:18.

193. A.D. 49. Ac 15:2, 6, 22. Cf. Gal 1:18. 2:10. Here James, Peter and John were called "pillars of the Church."

194. Ac 8:1. A.D. 36. Cf. Fitzmyer, *art. cit.,* p. 218.

195. 1 Tm 4:14.

196. Ac 1:8.

197. Ac 9:27 (Barnabas), 13:1–3 (Antioch).

198. Rm 1:1, Gal 1:15, 2 Cor 5:20.

199. 1 Cor 3:5, 9, 2 Cor 6:1.

200. 1 Cor 13:7, Eph 4:15–16. Cf. Hans von Campenhausen, *Kirchliches Amt und geistliche Vollmacht in den ersten drei Jahrhunderten* (Tübingen: Mohr, 1953), pp. 55–57.

201. 1 Cor 15:10. Cf. 1 Cor 1:17–18, 5, 7, 2 Cor 5:19–20.

202. Raymond E. Brown, *Priest and Bishop* (New York: Paulist, 1970), p. 59.

203. Rm 15:8.

204. 1 Cor 4:1.

205. McKenzie, *op. cit.,* p. 56 notes that the term is used more often in Paul of apostleship than it is used in the whole rest of the NT. Cf. Rm 11:13, 15:23, 31, 1 Cor 3:5, 2 Cor 3:3, 6, 4:1, 5:18, 6:3, 4, 8:4, 19, 11:8, 15, 23, Eph 3:7, Col 1:7, 23, 25, Phl 1:1.

206. 1 Cor 4:9–13, 2 Cor 11:23–28, Gal 6:17.

207. McKenzie, *op. cit.,* pp. 51, 53, 55. 1 Cor 6–8.

208. Brown, *Priest,* pp. 61–62. He cites the example of Paul, deciding for the admission of gentiles into the Church without circumcision on the basis of the meaning of Christ's death and resurrection, not on the basis of the mind or teaching of the historical Jesus.

209. Brown, *Priest,* p. 72.

210. 1 Pt 2:5, Rv 1:6, 5:10, 20:6.

211. Brown, *Priest,* pp. 13–14.

212. *Ibid.,* p. 14. 1 Pt 2:5, Rv 1:6, 5:10, 20:6.

213. John H. Elliott, *The Elect and the Holy, Novum Testamentum Supp.* XII (Leiden: Brill, 1966). Cited by Brown, *Priest,* p. 14.

214. 1 Cor 1:12–17.

215. Ac 2:46, 21:26 (the latter passage indicates that Paul himself went to the Temple c. 58 A.D.).

216. Brown, *Priest,* pp. 17–19.

217. Did 13–14, 1 Clem 40 (where it is connected with priesthood). Brown, *Priest,* p. 19, points out that this fact must modify "the claim that historically Jesus instituted the priesthood at the Last Supper."

218. Brown, *Priest,* pp. 21, 42–43, 45.

219. Rm 15:8.

220. Mk 10:45 pars.

221. Mk 9:35, 10:43–45, Mt 20:26–28, 23:11, 25:44–45, Lk 12:37, 22:26–27.

222. Phl 2:5–11.

223. Jn 12:26.

224. Ac 6:4.

225. Ac 20:24.

226. 2 Cor 5:18.

227. 2 Cor 3:6.

228. Eph 3:7, Col 1:23.

229. Col 1:25.

230. Ac 11:29 (famine relief), Rm 15:31 (collection for Jerusalem).

231. 1 Cor 12:9–10.

232. 1 Cor 12:5.

233. 1 Cor 3:5, 2 Cor 3:6, 6:4, 11:15, 23, Col 1:23, 25.

234. 1 Th 3:2 var. (Timothy), Col 1:7 (Epaphras), 4:7 (Tychicus).

235. Rm 12:6–7, Ac 20:24. Cf. 1 Cor 12:4–5.

236. Phl 1:1. This was written either from Ephesus c. 56–57 A.D., or from Rome between 61 and 63 A.D.

237. Eduard Schweizer, *Church Order in the New Testament* (London: S.C.M., 1961), p. 208.

238. Ac 6:5.

239. Ac 8:35, 40 (evangelizing), 21:8 (evangelist).

240. Brown, "Roles," p. 690, n. 8.

241. Phl 1:1.

242. E.-B. Allo, *Première épître aux Corinthiens* (Paris: Gabalda, 1956), p. 465, C.K. Barrett, *The First Epistle to the Corinthians* (New York: Harper & Row, 1968), p. 394, Jean Héring, *The First Epistle of St. Paul to the Corinthians* (London: Epworth, 1962), pp. 185–186, Hans Lietzmann, *An die Korinther I–II* (Tübingen: Mohr, 1931), p. 89.

243. H. W. Beyer, *"Diakonos,"* *TDNT* II, p. 90.

244. The office of deacon is not mentioned in Acts.

245. 1 Cor 12:12, 14:3, 5, 12, Eph 4:12, 16.

246. Rm 12:9, 1 Cor 13, Eph 4:15–16. Cf. Col 3:14.

247. 1 Cor 1:18, 5, 7.

248. 1 Cor 12:29.

249. Ac 21:9, 1 Cor 11:5.

250. 1 Cor 14:37–38.

251. 1 Cor 14:3, 31.

252. 1 Cor 13:2.
253. 1 Cor 12:7–11, 14:2, 30–33.
254. Rm 12:6.
255. 1 Cor 14:29.
256. 1 Cor 12:3, 14:5b, 12, 37–38.
257. *Eucharistein.* Did 10:7.
258. *Leitourgein.* Ac 13:1–2.
259. Did 15:1–2.
260. Ernst Haenchen, *The Acts of the Apostles* (Philadelphia: Westminster, 1971), p. 395.
261. 1 Cor 11:2, 23, 15:1, 3.
262. Cf. Haenchen, *op. cit.,* p. 395.
263. Rm 12:6–8, 1 Cor 12:28.
264. 1 Th 5:12.
265. Hb 13:7, 17, 24. Cf. 1 Clem 1:3, 21:6.
266. André Lemaire, "From Services to Ministries: *'Diakoniai'* in the First Two Centuries," *Concilium* 80 (1972), pp. 191–192. He notes that Harnack, on the other hand, had erroneously distinguished the two.
267. Joachim Jeremias, *Jerusalem in the Time of Jesus* (Philadelphia: Fortress, 1969), p. 261. Beyer, *TDNT* II, p. 618, Brown, *Priest,* p. 68.
268. Ac 20:17, 28. Brown, *Priest,* p. 65.
269. Tit 1:5, 7. Brown, *Priest,* pp. 65–66.
270. Brown, *Priest,* p. 72. Cf. pp. 68–72.
271. *Ibid.,* p. 37.
272. CD 13:9–10. Cf. Brown, *Priest,* pp. 67–68.
273. Brown, *Priest,* p. 68, n. 47. Josephus, *War* II, 123 (*cheirotonein*), Did 15:1.
274. 1 Pt 2:25.
275. 1 Tm 3:4–5, Tit 1:7, 9–10.
276. Ac 11:30, 15:2, 4, 6, 22–23, 16:4, 21:18.
277. Ac 11:30.
278. Ac 15:2, 4, 6, 22–23, 16:4.
279. Ac 21:18.
280. Such as Ephesus, Ac 20:17.
281. Ac 14:23.
282. Jas 5:14, 1 Pt 5:1–4.
283. Tit 1:5–9.

CHAPTER THREE:
THE MINISTRY OF WOMEN
ACCORDING TO
THE NEW TESTAMENT

This chapter will consider the New Testament evidence concerning the ministry of women in the time of Jesus and in the first century Church. The New Testament is a collection of writings of many different authors. Each New Testament writer or redactor was an historical human person with his own theological attitudes and ideas. Each was to some extent a product of the experience, both Christian and cultural, of a different historical community. All of the New Testament writers were men of the first century. Each had his own theological and cultural attitudes toward the position and role of women in the Church and in secular society. Each came out of a unique experience of the role of women in his own community.

There will be two major sections in this chapter. The first will consider the ministry of women during the historical lifetime of Jesus as it is presented by the four evangelists writing in the second half of the first century. It will discuss the information about the discipleship and ministerial role of women which is found in each of the gospels. In order to comprehend the differences among the four gospels it will be necessary to consider the theological attitude of each evangelist on the subject of the position and role of women. The second section of the chapter will discuss the various ministries exercised by women in the early Church during the New Testament period as these are portrayed in Acts and the epistles.

THE MINISTRY OF WOMEN DURING
THE LIFETIME OF JESUS

Discipleship

The disciples of Jesus, according to the gospels, were those persons who heard and responded to his call to follow him. The earliest evangelist, Mark, portrayed Jesus teaching about the nature of discipleship: "If anyone would come after me, let that person deny self, take up the cross and follow me."[1] The technical expression denoting discipleship in the gospels was the "following" of Jesus. All four gospels portrayed women as well as men following Jesus during his historical lifetime.

In the gospels the majority of disciples named were men. To be properly understood, this fact must be considered in the light of the contemporary cultural and religious situation. First of all the gospels were written by men who were the products of a culture which strongly emphasized the superior importance of men and the subordinate role of women.

Secondly, those writing within a Jewish milieu were affected by the dictum in rabbinic Judaism in the intertestamental period that women were not permitted to study Torah with a rabbi. Since the gospel did present Jesus as a rabbi at least during the earlier part of his ministry, it would have been quite difficult for a Jewish evangelist to portray women as rabbinic disciples receiving instruction from their teacher on an equal basis with men disciples. Matthew, the most Jewish of the gospels, pointed out most clearly the real distinction between discipleship of Jesus and rabbinic discipleship.[2] In the radical newness of Jesus' servant mode of discipleship women also could learn from him, follow him, serve and be his disciples.

During the period of the itinerant Galilean ministry there may also have been a problem with contemporary social convention. In the first century it was not socially acceptable for women to wander about the countryside following a male teacher and camping in the open in proximity to a group of men. Yet on the other hand, it was precisely this practice of Jesus of teaching in the open and not just in the synagogue that enabled women to be his disciples. If he had confined his teaching to synagogue and Temple, women would have been barred altogether from listening to him. The evangelists seem to have attempted to resolve the problem by acknowledging the presence of women who followed Jesus, but at the same time keeping these women in the background as much as possible.

In spite of these cultural and religious reasons to the contrary, the evangelists did portray women following Jesus throughout his historical lifetime. Each of the evangelists represents a different theological position, conditioned by his own time, place and situation. Therefore it is necessary to examine what each of the different gospel traditions had to say about the discipleship of women and to evaluate this in the light of each individual evangelist's own theological attitude toward women.

a. Mark. The first gospel to have been written was that of Mark. This gospel presents one of the earliest and most reliable traditions about the life and ministry of Jesus within the framework and theological understanding of the Markan evangelist. Matthew and Luke drew upon the Markan tradition as the primary source for their gospels, adding some material from other sources as well as their own theological reflection.

There are references to the presence of women during the ministry of Jesus throughout the Markan gospel, from the beginning of the Galilean ministry to the crucifixion. The first mention of women is in Mark 1:29–31. In context this pericope stands between the narrative of the call of the first four disciples and that of the call of Levi.[3] There is a series of four stories about healings between the two call narratives. The second such story is about the healing of Simon's mother-in-law. Jesus healed her by touch without fear of contracting ritual impurity through touching a woman. After she was healed, she "served" them. By the time of the evangelist the word "serve" (*diakonein*) was a technical term for the ministry of Christians.[4] The tradition behind this passage is, according to Vincent Taylor, early, probably handed down from Peter himself.[5]

Mark 3:31–35 describes a scene in which the mother and brothers or Jesus come and ask for him. Jesus thereupon teaches that his real mother and brothers and sisters are those who do the will of God, who are disciples of Jesus whose own ministry was to do the will of his Father.[6] It is striking that the evangelist explicitly mentioned "sisters." Elsewhere in the New Testament "brothers" is sometimes used generically to denote both men and women. In the first part of the scene in this passage only "mother and brothers" were mentioned.[7] It is extremely unlikely that the evangelist would have added the reference to women among the disciples unless it were strongly rooted in the tradition and also known to the Christian community for which he was writing.

Mark 6:3 mentions the presence of Jesus' sisters in Nazareth. This verse and the one described above have been understood to mean that Mary and the brothers of Jesus were no longer in Nazareth,[8] but were following Jesus. This should be considered in conjunction with other passages which refer to the discipleship of Mary.

Between the two scenes of the story of the healing of a twelve-year-old girl, Mark inserted the story of the healing of the woman with a hemorrhage.[9] This was not explicitly a story about discipleship, but it did portray a woman talking with Jesus face to face. She was presented by the evangelist as a paradigm of understanding and of faith, in contrast to the inner circle of men disciples who throughout the gospel are presented as lacking in understanding and belief. Both faith and understanding of who Jesus is are important characteristics of true discipleship in the gospel of Mark.

The story of the Syrophoenician woman in Mark 7:24–30 portrays a hellenistic gentile woman holding her own in a discussion with Jesus. Jesus recognized the validity of her argument and on that basis granted her request for the healing of her daughter. Taylor finds many details of this story quite primitive, and considers that it was based on an early and reliable tradition.[10] This woman also is presented as an example of faith, of understanding and belief that Jesus through his lordship was able to heal even at a distance and even those who were not members of the people of Israel. Although both a woman and a gentile, the Syrophoenician woman showed greater understanding than the inner circle of disciples.

Mark 10:28–30 described Jesus' teaching on the rewards that will come to those who leave everything and follow him. Two types of reward are distinguished: those which will come in this life, which are fellowship with the true family of disciples and persecutions, and those of the age to come which will be eternal life. In the community of Jesus' disciples on earth there will be "brothers and sisters and mothers and children." It presumes that both women and men serve

Jesus and each other on an equal basis.[11] This passage also implies
that women and men will participate equally in the kingdom of God.

Mark 12:41–43 portrays Jesus presenting a poor widow to the
disciples as a paradigm of generosity and total giving of all one's possessions. Elsewhere in Mark it was precisely the demand for total re-
nunciation of possessions which had been shown to be an obstacle to
discipleship for some, especially the rich.[12] The story of the poor widow is immediately preceded by a teaching of Jesus in which he was
said to have criticized the scribes for exploiting helpless women
while at the same time engaging in ostentatious religious practices.
Such men would in the long run be condemned.

The passion narrative is the oldest and most reliable section of
the gospels. Mark 14:3–9 presents the story of the anointing of Jesus
by an unnamed woman. In the johannine version of the story the
woman is said to have been Mary, the sister of Lazarus, whose discipleship will be discussed below. It is possible to conjecture at this
point that the woman was a disciple since she knew who and where
Jesus was, in the house of Simon the leper at Bethany, and she understood that Jesus was approaching a critical moment in his life for
which she was helping to prepare him through her anointing. In the
Old Testament, anointing had been the function of elders, prophets
and priests,[13] all of which, although different, were important forms
of religious office.

In the Markan passage the disciples reproached the woman for
wasting such expensive ointment, since it might have been sold and
its price given to the poor. This note may also be taken to support
the notion of the woman's discipleship, since during the ministry of
Jesus the disciples pooled their resources and therefrom gave alms to
the poor. If she were a disciple, her money would have been available
to the community for alms distribution.

The action of this woman did serve as a witness to Jesus' true
identity and to his destiny of suffering, which throughout the gospel
of Mark had been a major theme, coupled with the disciples' lack of
understanding of precisely these points. The evangelist also added
the statement in verse 9 connecting the woman's act of witness here
with the later proclamation of the gospel to the whole world by the
Church. Thus the evangelist implicitly presented the role of the

woman in terms of the ministry of witness of the disciple or apostle of Jesus.

The last two verses of the crucifixion narrative in Mark 15:40–41 describe the women who were present. Mary of Magdala, Mary the mother of James the Younger and of Joses, and Salome are mentioned by name. These women are characterized through the use of two verbs, both of which were technical terms in the vocabulary of discipleship and ministry in the New Testament: they "followed" (*akolouthein*) Jesus and "served" (*diakonein*) him. This was equivalent to calling the women "disciples" and "ministers." Further on, in verse 41b, reference was made to "many other women who came up with him to Jerusalem." The verb "to come up with" (*synanabainein*) also denoted a formal accompanying of Jesus. It is used again in Acts 13:31 where it served to connect those who had come up with Jesus to the witnessing of his resurrection appearances and the commission to ministry:

> "And for many days he appeared to those who came up
> with him from Galilee to Jerusalem, who are now his wit-
> nesses to the people."

As will be demonstrated later in the section dealing with apostleship, this was equivalent to calling these persons "apostles." In Mark 15 it served to underscore the discipleship of the women.

The crucifixion is the first of three final scenes of the tableau of Jesus' life. In all of these scenes women are named as prominent witnesses. The other two scenes are the burial and the resurrection. In the Markan burial scene, Mary of Magdala and Mary of James are mentioned by name. The only other character in the scene was Joseph of Arimathea who was the agent of burial. The witnesses of the burial were the women. This scene reinforced the portrayal of the fidelity of the women disciples in accompanying Jesus to the very end, as opposed to the men disciples who were not mentioned by Mark as present either at the crucifixion or at the tomb.

The original gospel of Mark ended with the story of the empty tomb (Mark 16:1–8). It was only the women who came to the tomb. Mary of Magdala, Mary of James, and Salome are mentioned by name. It was these women who were the first to see that the tomb was empty. It was they who were addressed by the angelic figure who told them that Jesus was risen and commissioned them to go and bear witness of the resurrection to the other disciples and to Peter. It is not clear in the original ending of Mark whether the women carried out their mission. Mark makes note of their fear and hesitancy. The other three gospels as well as the secondary ending of Mark do portray the women, or at least Mary of Magdala, as fulfilling the commission and bearing witness of the resurrection to the other disciples.[14]

Thus the gospel of Mark does indicate that women were among the disciples of Jesus. It also demonstrates several times that, because of their faith, understanding and fidelity, the discipleship of the women was paradigmatic for the men, who exhibited a lack of all three qualities which were essential for true discipleship. This was the theological interpretation of the evangelist, but it was based upon data from the earliest stratum of tradition about the life and ministry of Jesus.

b. Matthew. Matthew was composed in a Jewish-Christian milieu for the purpose of demonstrating to the Jews of the pharisaic-rabbinic tradition that Jesus was the Messiah, the fulfillment of the law and the prophets. The author showed great familiarity with the Old Testament, which he cited more than any other evangelist, and with the modes of thought and methods of argument of rabbinic Judaism. Matthew was written later than Mark and was dependent upon the latter, although the author also used other sources. Matthew reproduced most of the references to women which were found in Mark, although with some editorial alterations. He did not add any other references to women from his other sources, whether as disciples or as characters in parables or miracle stories. This stands in strong contrast to Luke who added a great amount of material about women beyond that contained in the Markan tradition.

Many of the Markan stories about women are greatly abbreviated in Matthew. This reluctance to note the presence of women around Jesus, the great rabbi, was consistent with Matthew's method of arguing from within the traditions of rabbinic Judaism, which at that time totally excluded women from rabbinic schooling. It was also consistent with the influence of the Old Testament which warned of the contaminating effect of women which could render a man ritually impure.

Matthew 8:14–15 presents the healing of Peter's mother-in-law in barest outline. It did preserve from the tradition the fact that Jesus touched the woman and that she "served." Yet it changed the object of her service from the plural "them," denoting the whole community, to the singular, Jesus.

The story of the woman with the hemorrhage is likewise greatly shortened. In Matthew 9:20–23 the active role of the woman in speaking intelligently with Jesus is omitted, as is also mention of her understanding of Jesus' identity and his power to heal. The reference to her faith in the final saying of Jesus has, however, been retained.

The story of the Syrophoenician woman is retold in Matthew 15:21–28. In this version the woman is called a "Canaanite" which, to the Jewish mind schooled in the Old Testament, would sound derogatory. The Markan note that she was Syrophoenician and Greek, which connoted a higher level of education and culture, was omitted. The woman's initial part in the dialogue is reduced by Matthew to a single phrase, although the final interchange with Jesus is preserved almost intact. Matthew also added a reference to the greatness of her faith, possibly to justify his inclusion of a story about a gentile woman.

The Markan saying about disciples receiving new brothers and sisters and mothers while following Jesus is omitted, even though the preceding and the subsequent phrases of its context are preserved.[15]

The Matthean passion narrative recounts the story of the anointing at Bethany but in somewhat abbreviated form.[16] The crucifixion narrative mentions the presence of Mary of Magdala, Mary the mother of James and Joseph, and the mother of the sons of Zebedee. It also notes the presence of many other women "who had followed Jesus from Galilee, ministering to him."[17] Thus Matthew has preserved the Markan tradition of the women disciples. He has applied the verbs "follow" and "serve" to all of the women, thus expanding and confirming their discipleship. Mark had used these technical terms only of the three women whom he named, designating them as disciples, whereas the other women were less clearly disciples in the technical sense. This is one of the few instances where Matthew went beyond the Markan tradition in his portrayal of the role of women.

The Matthean burial account notes the presence of Mary of Magdala and "the other Mary" as witnesses. Matthew continues to follow the Markan tradition in presenting Mary of Magdala and another Mary as witnesses of the empty tomb and recipients of an angelic commission. Yet Matthew tempers the women's fear with joy and portrays them "running" to tell the other disciples of the resurrection. Then, in a scene which is unique to Matthew, there is an initial resurrection appearance of Jesus to the women on the road. The response of the women is recognition and worship. Then Jesus is portrayed as formally commissioning them to go and tell the men disciples.[18] It is extremely unlikely that Matthew would have invented the story of an initial appearance of Jesus to women. In fact, given his consistent mode of dealing with stories about women elsewhere in his gospel, he would have been more likely to have omitted it. Thus for such a story to have been retained in Matthew's gospel it must have been based upon irrefutable tradition which was known to Matthew's community. This same tradition is also found in the secondary ending of Mark and in the johannine resurrection narrative.

Of all the gospels, Matthew gives the most prominent role to the Twelve. Many times at various points in the gospel narrative he mentions the special mission of the Twelve.[19] For Matthew's argument the nation of Israel was of very great importance, and Israel, according to Jewish law, was constituted only by its male members. Thus it was consistent for the evangelist to emphasize both the male constituents of Israel and to attempt to minimize the presence and role of women among the disciples of Jesus and in the early Christian community. For those who stood within the tradition of contemporary rabbinic Judaism, women could play no official role in religious affairs. And the mere presence of women could render the men ritually impure. Therefore the logical conclusion was to avoid as much as possible any mention of women. Within such a milieu it is remarkable that women were in fact mentioned in the gospel of Matthew. This attests to the strength of the tradition of the discipleship of women and the fact of women being the primary witnesses of the resurrection and recipients of the risen Jesus' commission to ministry. It also attests to the probable situation that women did play a ministerial role in the late first-century community of the evangelist. Thus Matthew was unable to ignore the presence of women disciples of Jesus when he wrote his gospel.

c. The Writings of Luke. The theological perspectives of the third evangelist also determined his presentation of the Markan tradition and of his material from other sources. According to Hans Conzelmann, the history of salvation was, for Luke, divided into three eras.[20] The first was the period of Israel, from Moses and the prophets through John the Baptist. The second was the period of the historical ministry of Jesus, beginning with the temptation narrative in Luke 4 and continuing through the ascension. The third period was that of the Church, which would last from the time of Pentecost until the parousia. It was within this third age that Luke himself wrote his gospel for Christians who were also living within this time.

In studying the discipleship of women within the Lukan corpus, it becomes evident that the status and role of women are greatest in the period of Israel, much less during the ministry of Jesus and quite restricted in the period of the Church. The reason for this lay in Luke's theology and in his own position toward women. It would seem that women had an important and active role in Luke's own late first-century community. This was such that he could not ignore the importance of women altogether, but, reacting negatively to their present active role, he could, through the theology of his gospel, attempt to argue for the restriction of women's role in the Church of his day.[21]

In the infancy narratives of Luke 1–2, which are distinct from the rest of the gospel, the evangelist presents three parallel tableaux of the annunciation, birth and naming of John the Baptist and of Jesus. In the John the Baptist scenes, the dominant character is Elizabeth. In the Jesus scenes the dominant character is Mary. The two women are brought together in an intermediary episode portraying the visitation.

The role of Elizabeth is less than that of Mary's. She is paired with Zechariah who, unlike Joseph, played an active role. It was Zechariah who, according to Luke, received the annunciation of John's birth and who proclaimed the final hymn of praise and thanksgiving in response to it. Yet during the heart of the scene it was Elizabeth who was the dominant character, while Zechariah was unable to speak at all. It was Elizabeth who carried her child in faith and who, contrary to Jewish custom, bestowed upon him his name.

In the scene of the visitation the two women characters, Mary and Elizabeth, meet face to face. Mary is shown to be a paradigm of the person of faith, although this is still the faith of Israel. Her faith is proclaimed through Elizabeth's recognition: "blessed is she who believed."[22] The climax of the scene is Mary's proclamation of the magnificat. Both characters in this scene are women of faith. Through her own faith Elizabeth recognized and bore witness to the faith of Mary. And Mary in faith bore witness to the saving actions of God.[23]

On the other side of the diptych Mary herself received the annunciation of Jesus' birth in obedience of faith. When he was born she kept all her thoughts in her heart. In so doing she is again portrayed as an example of obedient faith. But even this faith in the incarnation of the redeemer is, for Luke, still the faith of Israel. Christian faith will be the post-resurrectional faith of the Church.

In the final scene depicting the infancy of Jesus, he was presented in the Temple as his mother was purified after childbirth. Two new characters are introduced in this scene: Simeon and Anna. Simeon is the dominant figure. He is mentioned first and the text of his two prophetic utterances is given. The character and actions of Anna are described in the third person, but she herself does not speak according to the Lukan narrative. The character of Anna bears a striking resemblance to the Christian widows of the late first century. Luke notes her age, which was eighty-four, that she worshiped in the Temple with prayer and fasting day and night, and that she had been married only once, remaining celibate after the death of her husband. In 1 Timothy 5 the qualifications listed for enrollment as a Christian widow are that the person be more than sixty years old and married only once, spend night and day in prayer and supplication, and be known for good deeds and service of the Church.[24] Thus in his composition of the character of Anna, Luke actually may have been writing about Christian widows who were active in the Church in his own time.

The following scene, which concludes the infancy narrative, describes the visit to the Temple when Jesus was twelve years old. The picture of Mary in this scene is complex. Mary is more prominent than Joseph. In 2:48 she speaks for both parents. Yet her question betrays her lack of understanding. On the one hand, Luke repeats the saying from the birth scene that she kept all these things in her heart. This seems to point to her faith and understanding. Yet in the preceding verse (2:50) it is noted that neither parent understood Jesus' saying that he had been in his Father's house. It is possible that Luke was pointing out that their faith, and the faith of Israel, were incomplete.

Thus for Luke, in the period of Israel, it was possible for women to be examples of faith, and to exercise a ministry of proclamation of the word. It must be kept in mind that these women bore witness to the faith of Israel, not to Christian faith. Luke did not make a connection between the role of women before the time of Jesus and their role within the Christian economy. According to Conzelmann, in Luke's understanding of salvation history, the ministries of the earlier periods could not be repeated and could not serve as models for the period of the Church.[25]

Toward the end of his section of the Galilean ministry of Jesus Luke first explicitly mentions the presence of women among the disciples. He mentions by name Mary of Magdala, Joanna the wife of Chuza, Herod's steward, and Susanna. He also noted that there were many others.[26] However, Luke characteristically qualified every mention of women by a reference to some negative aspect of their character. Here he noted that these women had been healed of evil spirits and infirmities, especially Mary of Magdala from whom seven demons had been cast out. This is a literary device used throughout the gospel of Luke to present women as both weak and sinful. Luke also describes the role of the woman as providing for Jesus and the Twelve materially. This is likewise a Lukan device, found in a number of passages, to restrict the ministry of women to one of providing financial aid, omitting any reference to women exercising a ministry of proclamation. This passage is found only in the gospel of Luke.

In this same chapter the Lukan version of the saying of Jesus about his true relations omits any reference to "sisters" although this had appeared in both the Markan and Matthean versions. "Sisters" in this context meant members of the Christian community, not siblings of Jesus. In Luke, the disciples, or hearers of the word do not replace the mother and brothers of Jesus as his true family. Rather his mother and brothers are part of the true family of disciples because they hear the word and do it.[27] Thus although Luke in this passage is attempting to omit the presence of women in general among the disciples, he cannot avoid affirming the presence of at least one woman, Mary. This is confirmed by his mention of Mary among the disciples again in Acts 1:14.

One exception to the general restriction of the role of women in the third gospel is the story of the healing of the woman with the hemorrhage in Luke 8:43–48. Luke alone gave the woman a role of proclaiming what had taken place to the people. She understood what had happened and was able to explain it to the people. In a final blessing Jesus is portrayed as commending her for her faith. Yet her faith was also not Christian faith in the complete sense for it was pre-resurrectional.

The domestic story of Mary and Martha in Luke 10:38–42 is found only in the third gospel. The entire tenth chapter of Luke discusses the theme of discipleship. It is not denied that Mary and Martha are disciples. The focus is on the actual roles of each of these women. The role of Mary is one of listening and learning. The role of Martha is that of serving the men. Thus Luke was portraying the role of serving or ministry for women as subordinate to the role of listening. Luke did go beyond contemporary rabbinic Judaism in permitting a woman to learn Torah. By her listening Mary was a disciple in the Jewish sense. But Luke did not permit either of the women a role of proclamation. It is possible that Martha represents the women ministers who were active in Luke's own church. Thus in his composition of this scene the evangelist was attempting to limit and subordinate the ministerial role of such women by appealing to the example of Jesus. These two women characters are portrayed quite differently in the fourth gospel.

Another brief pericope which is unique to Luke is 11:27–28. Here an unnamed woman raised her voice above the crowd in an attempt at proclaiming the beatitude of Jesus' physical mother. But Luke then presented Jesus as correcting her mistake. As in the pericope on the true family of Jesus, it is the disciples who believe and keep the word of God who are truly blessed. This has been understood as reaffirming the discipleship of Mary.[28]

In the other gospels, the story of the anointing of Jesus stood in a climactic position immediately before the last supper. Luke placed it within the Galilean ministry. He reproduced the basic story from the Markan tradition, but added the detail that the woman was a sinner. He mentioned this bit of information five times within the story, noting also that her sins were many.[29]

Luke retained the story of the poor widow, which Matthew had omitted. According to the Markan tradition she was an example of generosity characteristic of true Christian service. It is possible that Luke's reason for retaining the story was connected with the role of widows in his own church whom he may have been trying to influence through his writings. The one role of women which Luke could affirm without qualification was that of giving alms.

In the passion narrative Luke alone notes the presence of women along the way of the cross. He portrayed Jesus as addressing them in a brief apocalyptic discourse. The role of the women was one of listening, and also of wailing and lamenting.

Luke added the presence of men in his account of the crucifixion. Luke 24:49 states that "all who had known him and the women who had followed him from Galilee stood at a distance and saw these things." With the use of the word "all" Luke seems to be implying that the Eleven and perhaps other male disciples were present. At the same time Luke minimized the Markan tradition of the women by not mentioning any of the women by name, as the other three gospels did. Luke did, however, use the verb "follow" (*synakolouthein*) of the women which implied their discipleship.[30] In the burial account Luke likewise omitted the names of specific women, but did acknowledge that women were there.

In the resurrection narrative Luke began his account of the empty tomb without mentioning the women by name, although he added the names of Mary of Magdala, Joanna, and Mary the mother of James at the end. He affirmed that the women did report the empty tomb to the other disciples, but noted that the men did not believe them. Luke is the only one of the four gospels to omit an account of an initial resurrection appearance to women and a personal commissioning of women by the risen Jesus. What Luke reported instead was a story of an appearance to two persons on the road to Emmaus, in which the report of the women about the empty tomb was confirmed, and reference was made to an earlier appearance to Simon.[31] Finally, Luke presented the risen Jesus appearing to the company of the Eleven "and those who were with them" in Jerusalem. According to Acts 1:14 this group assembled in the upper room in Jerusalem did include the women, but Luke avoided any explicit mention of them in his resurrection narrative. If the women were indeed present then they too received the commission to proclamation and witness.[32] But Luke preferred to leave the point in ambiguity, just as throughout his gospel he made reference to "people," the "crowd," or the "multitude" accompanying Jesus. Such a group presumably included women, but Luke never made explicit mention of their presence unless the tradition made it unavoidable.

Another interesting phenomenon in the gospel of Luke is the pairing of healing stories and parables about men and women. Often these were traditions which were unique to Luke or else a single story or parable from the common tradition was expanded by the addition of a second story or parable about a woman. There are parallel healing stories about the centurion and the widow of Nain in Luke 7, and about sabbath healings of a crippled woman and a man with dropsy in Luke 13–14. There are also parallel parables of the kingdom about the mustard seed of the man and the leaven of the woman in Luke 13, of the man's lost sheep and the woman's lost coin in 15, and of the widow before the judge and the men in the Temple in 18. It has been suggested that this use of parallel stories about men and women reflected the catechetical situation in Luke's own church in the latter part of the first century, where women had a formative role in the catechetical mission and therefore had need of stories about women that they could use in their catechesis.[33]

Luke's attitude toward women is reaffirmed in the book of Acts, the second part of Luke's two-part work. There Luke frequently mentioned the presence of women among the baptized.[34] Yet he avoided mention of women active in the official ministry of the Church. Implicitly Luke allowed for the possibility of the presence of women at Pentecost. He had noted their presence in the upper room with the Eleven immediately before Pentecost and made no mention of the women leaving.[35] The sermon of Peter served to interpret the event of Pentecost for the people. Luke had Peter cite a passage from Joel which mentioned the pouring out of the Spirit upon "sons and daughters," "menservants and maidservants."[36] Luke's inclusion of this quotation suggests that women were in fact present at Pentecost and that this was well known to his readers. Pentecost was the event of the birth of the Church, the beginning of the third and final era in Luke's theology of history. It was also the event of the empowering of the members of the Christian community for mission. Thus it is of great theological importance whether women were present at this event as a basis for their full participation in the subsequent mission of the church. It is also significant that Luke never again mentions Mary after Acts 1:14. He gave her no role during the period of the Church. This may have been a result of his theological position on the role of women in the Church. It may also simply have been due to lack of historical information.[37]

In the period of the Church men were for Luke far more important than women. The dominant characters in Acts are all men, and chief among them are Peter and Paul. Luke presented the full text of many speeches and sermons of these men. The actual words of these sermons may reflect more Lukan composition than what was actually said on the occasion. Most of the sermons attributed to Peter and Paul in Acts begin with the phrases "men of Israel" or "men, brothers."[38] Likewise the speech of Stephen before his martyrdom began with the words "men, brothers and fathers."[39] The use of such language reflected Luke's own attitude toward women.

In Acts as in the third gospel Luke focused on the passive role of women. Women believed, prayed and were the objects of healing.[40] Sometimes Luke introduced women characters into a dramatic scene to demonstrate the superiority of a male apostle, such as Peter.[41] Luke also emphasized the sinfulness of one married couple, Ananias and Sapphira, in contrast to the righteous authority of Peter.[42] He mentioned the women of high standing in Antioch of Pisidia who, together with the men of the city, incited the persecution of Paul and of the Christian community.[43] Roman women, however, were mentioned by Luke without criticism. The wives of corrupt Roman officials were probably open to a great deal of criticism, but Luke in his effort to justify Christianity to a Roman audience, never hinted at any censure of Roman women.[44]

The primary role of Christian women according to Acts was to provide material support for the male apostles or a place of worship for the Christian community.[45] Only three times in Acts did Luke mention women who were prominent in the ministry of the Church. In the first instance, the hellenist leader Philip had four daughters who prophesied.[46] The fact that Luke mentioned these women at all was probably because they were well known in the Church. The way in which he described them tended to minimize their importance. He avoided the official title of "prophet," using a verbal reference to their prophetic activity instead. He also noted that they were unmarried. The tone of this verse is that of a late first-century man who was uncomfortable with any reference to women holding ecclesiastical office and who, if he was unable to deny the reality of these historical women, at least was able to interject his opinion that only celibate women should be permitted in ministry.

The second reference in Acts to a woman in ministry was to the married couple, Priscilla and Aquila. The description of their activity also seems to have been minimized in Acts in contrast to other references to them in Paul's letters.[46B] Acts mentioned only that Paul sought them out and stayed at their house, and that later they accompanied Paul as far as Ephesus.[47] Acts 18:26 stands as a striking exception to the previous low-key presentation of the couple. There it is noted that they instructed the missionary apostle Apollos, since they understood Christian teaching more accurately than he. Thus in this one verse Luke permits a glimpse of a woman exercising a ministry of word, even to the point of being the teacher of a prominent male missionary apostle. It may also be significant that two times out of the three that the names of the couple are mentioned, that of Priscilla is mentioned first. This was contrary to the normal usage of the time and may indicate that she was considered more important in the Church's ministry than her husband.

The third woman prominent in the ministerial life of the Church was Tabitha (or Dorcas in Greek). Acts 9:36 explicitly states that she was a disciple. This is the only occurrence of the feminine form of the word "disciple" in the New Testament.[47B] It is striking that the context does not call other characters disciples, such as Aeneas in the preceding healing story or the two men who were sent to fetch Peter. Only Tabitha and the men who seemed to hold authority in her community were called disciples.

The precise ministry of Tabitha is unclear. It was stated that she had done many good works and acts of mercy. In verse 39 it is mentioned that she had been with the widows making clothes. Because of the number of her own ministerial works it is probable that she herself was not a widow but was engaged rather in helping them. The scant evidence of the role of widows at this time would indicate that it was more passive, that they were more the recipients than the givers of aid and service. At any rate the presence of the widows at the deathbed and the sending for Peter to come from Lydda to Jaffa indicated that Tabitha was considered both important and beloved by her community. It is noteworthy that the only person to be raised from the dead by an apostle was a woman. There is little Lukan editing in this passage which simply presents the story as it was found in tradition.[48]

Elisabeth S. Fiorenza may be quite correct in her suggestion[49] that the role of women in the church of Luke may have been far greater than what was revealed in Acts and that both in the third gospel and in Acts, the Lukan redactor was intentionally seeking to minimize the discipleship and apostolic activity of women, even to the extent of altering the tradition he had received. Luke-Acts seems to reflect a situation in the Church similar to that found in the pastoral epistles near the end of the first century. Women had long been free to exercise a major and influential role in the ministry of the Church. But by this time the men were becoming weary of this situation and were seeking to keep women quiet within the community and to restrict their role to a passive one, although they were still eager to benefit materially from the resources of well-to-do women. In the light of this understanding of the theological position of Luke toward women, it is possible to comprehend more exactly the minimal evidence of the discipleship of women in the third gospel and to understand it in the light of the Lukan redaction and composition. Even a writer with such a restrictive attitude toward the role of women as Luke was unable to obliterate the record of the historical discipleship and official ecclesiastical ministry of women from the tradition.

d. John. The fourth gospel is not dependent upon the synoptic gospels or upon their traditions. It drew upon comparably reliable and primitive traditions of its own. It included accurate historical information about Jesus and his times not found in any other gospel.

Like the other gospels, however, its presentation of the history of Jesus is colored by its theological concern with the deeper meaning of that history. This concern dominates the literary structure of the gospel.[50]

The gospel of John, after a prologue, begins with an introductory section in which John the Baptist and two pairs of disciples, Andrew and Peter, Philip and Nathanael, prophetically bear witness to the identity of Jesus. The call narratives of these disciples are exemplaric, showing the nature of discipleship as following Jesus and seeing, believing and witnessing to who Jesus is. John made no attempt to present stories of the call of each member of the Twelve. For John discipleship was the important category, not the Twelve, an institution which by the time of his redaction of the gospel had disappeared from the Church.

The first half of the fourth gospel is a "Book of Signs."[51] It is structured around seven miraculous signs of Jesus' glory. The first and last of these included women. The first sign is the story of the wedding at Cana. The mother of Jesus was present, invited separately from Jesus, probably because she was acquainted with the family of the bride or groom. John presented Jesus dissociating himself from her personal request and addressing her as "woman" rather then "mother." This will be characteristic of the role of Mary later in the gospel. She is important in John because she is Jesus' disciple, not because she is his mother.[52] The verse which immediately follows the Cana scene (2:12) shows Mary accompanying Jesus and the other disciples to Capernaum.

Toward the end of the gospel and framing the johannine portrait of the historical life of Jesus, John again presented Mary in the role of disciple in the scene of the crucifixion.[53] According to Raymond Brown,[54] the figures in John who are most symbolic of Christian discipleship are Mary and the "beloved disciple." Neither one is called by his or her proper name in the fourth gospel. The two are brought together in the scene at the cross. Mary is given the role of mother to the beloved disciple, thus becoming part of Jesus' true family through her discipleship. At the same time the evangelist showed the beloved disciple becoming Jesus' true brother through his discipleship. Mary and the beloved disciple stand together in the scene as disciples and as equals.

The second woman to appear in the Book of Signs is the Samaritan woman in John 4. The preceding chapters have shown a movement to ever more adequate belief in Jesus, from the Jews to Nicodemus to the Samaritan woman.[55] The Samaritan woman comes to the threshold of understanding that Jesus is the messiah.[56] But unlike the women presented in the third gospel, her role does not end with believing. She is portrayed as proclaiming and bearing witness to Jesus.[57] According to the fourth evangelist, the people "believed through her word."[58] This phrase recurs in Jesus' prayer for his disciples in the last supper discourse. "I do not pray for these only, but also for those who believe in me through their word."[59] Thus the disciple for John is the person who brings others to belief in Jesus through the witness of the word.

Brown has suggested that the missionary function of the Samaritan woman is underscored by the use of the technical verb "I send you" (apostellein) immediately before the affirmation of the fruitfulness of her witness in the following verse.[60] This woman disciple has prepared the harvest which the apostles will later reap. Thus the fourth evangelist seems to be suggesting that women may have played a role in the Samaritan mission and in the founding of churches. The reaction of the male disciples to Jesus' self-manifestation to the Samaritan woman and to her role of witnessing is portrayed by the evangelist as one of "shock." This reaction seems to be more to the fact that she was a woman than to the fact that she was a Samaritan.[61]

The final sign at the close of the Book of Signs is the scene of the raising of Lazarus. In this series of tableaux in John 11–12, the primary characters are women, Mary and Martha. Lazarus himself is completely passive, first ill, then dead. Discipleship for the fourth evangelist meant following Jesus and this involved understanding and believing who he is. There has been dramatic progression in seeing, understanding and believing throughout the Book of Signs. The climax of this progression is the confession of Martha in 11:27: "Yes, Lord, I believe that you are the Christ, the Son of God." The importance of her confession is illustrated by the fact that the final climactic verse of the gospel (20:31) states that the purpose for which the entire gospel was written was to help the reader to believe "that Jesus is the Christ, the Son of God, and that believing you may have life in his name." The context in which the confession of Martha was made was an important discourse of Jesus in which he revealed himself as the source of life.[62]

In the fourth gospel the confession of Martha takes the place of that of Peter at Caesarea Philippi in the synoptics.[63] In the synoptic gospels the confession scene serves to underscore the primacy of Peter in apostolic authority. The gospel of John begins and ends with the proclamation of Jesus as the Messiah and the Son of God.[64] The solemn confession of Martha that Jesus is Messiah and Son of God is the climactic midpoint of the gospel. In this scene the most important role of discipleship according to johannine theology, that of proclamation of Jesus' true identity, is given to a woman. Since the fourth gospel was written on two levels, that of the time of the historical Jesus and that of the time of the johannine community, Martha is thus also portrayed by the evangelist as a focal point of apostolic authority in the johannine community.

The disciple *par excellence,* according to many commentators, in the fourth gospel where discipleship is such an important category, is called only "the beloved disciple" or "the disciple whom Jesus loved." His identity has always been a mystery to interpreters, who agree only in presuming that he was a man. Some have identified him with John the evangelist, others with Lazarus, who was the only man named in the gospel as an object of Jesus' love.[65] Yet two verses later, the evangelist stated that Jesus "loved Martha, and her sister and Lazarus." Lazarus here was mentioned last. It was unusual in literature of the time for women to be mentioned before a man. This verse would imply that the women, or at least Martha, was better known to the evangelist. In the introduction to the section Lazarus is identified by his relationship to Mary and Martha.[66]

After Martha's confession the first thing she did was to go and call her sister Mary to come to Jesus. This action reflects the literary structure of the call narratives in John 1, where, after Andrew believed, he immediately went and called Simon Peter to come to Jesus. In the second call scene, when Jesus called Philip, his first act as a disciple was to call Nathanael to come to Jesus. In the fourth gospel literary structure is a theological tool of the evangelist. Here it serves to affirm the discipleship of Martha.

The final tableau in the drama at Bethany (12:1–8) begins with a reference to Martha serving at a meal. Brown has suggested that this passage reflects the usage of the verb "serve" (*diakonein*) in the time of the evangelist, when it denoted an official ministry of the Church.[67] The scene suggests eucharistic overtones since the context was set on Sunday, the day of eucharistic celebration in the johannine community.[68] It is noteworthy that the ministers at the meal were both women.

The scene concluded with the story of the anointing of Jesus. John placed the action immediately before the last supper and named the agent as Mary of Bethany. In the passage the evangelist contrasted the faithful service of Mary with the dishonesty of Judas. Her act is presented as a sign of her understanding of the nature of the hour which Jesus was approaching. When the disciple Judas criticized Mary's ministry Jesus defended it and admonished him to "let her alone" (12:7). Thus Mary is portrayed by the fourth evangelist as more truly a disciple than Judas, although the latter was one of the Twelve.

The Book of Signs concludes with the anointing of the feet of Jesus by Mary, the true disciple, contrasted with Judas, the thief and betrayer. In the following chapter (13) the Book of Glory opens with the scene in which Jesus washes the disciples' feet. Here too the faithful ministry of Jesus is contrasted with the infidelity of Judas. Thus the ministry of Mary is shown to be authentic because it parallels the ministry of Jesus. This becomes explicit in 13:12–17. Jesus is portrayed explaining the nature of ministry and using the image of servant:

> If I then, your Lord and Teacher, have washed your feet,
> you also ought to wash one another's feet. For I have given
> you an example, that you also should do as I have done to
> you (13:14–15, RSV).

The importance of the example of Mary, who anticipated and fulfilled the authentic mode of ministry of the true disciple of Jesus, is highlighted by its structural position, bridging the two halves of the gospel.

An equally important woman disciple in the fourth gospel was Mary of Magdala. She was named as present at the crucifixion, along with the mother of Jesus, her sister and Mary the wife of Clopas.[69] In the resurrection narrative, Mary of Magdala is the chief character. The other women are not mentioned, not because they were not present, but because it is a characteristic literary device in the fourth gospel to drop unessential characters in order to heighten dramatic tension within scenes.[70]

In John 20 the belief of Mary of Magdala is strikingly contrasted with Peter's lack of belief. According to John it was Peter and the beloved disciple who entered the empty tomb first. Peter saw the linen cloths, but did not believe. The beloved disciple saw and believed. Both had come to the tomb because of Mary of Magdala's testimony that it was empty.[71] But then the men went back home.

It was to Mary of Magdala that the risen Jesus first appeared.[72] When he called her by name, "Mary," she recognized who he was. In an earlier discourse in John 10 the fourth evangelist presented Jesus speaking about himself in the image of the good shepherd and of his disciples as sheep. "I am the good shepherd; I know my own and my own know me."[73] In the fourth gospel Jesus' "own" is a technical term for his disciples.[74] In the good shepherd passage the shepherd's "own" recognize him because he calls them by name. In the resurrection narrative it was when Jesus called Mary by name that she recognized him.[75] After the good shepherd called his own by name, he led them forth.[76] In the resurrection narrative after Mary recognized the risen Jesus, he commissioned her to go and bear witness to the other disciples.

It is significant that the fourth evangelist included Mary of Magdala among Jesus' "own," since it was his own who were, according to John 13:1, present at the last supper. In the last supper discourses John presented Jesus comparing his disciples to women in labor.[77] The company who were present at the last supper were called both Jesus' "own" and "little children."[78] The latter expression is characteristic in the johannine epistles where it denotes those men and women who believe in Jesus. The word itself, teknia, in Greek is neuter, meaning "children" without reference to their sex.[79] The climax of the last supper scene in John 13:35 gives a typical johannine description of discipleship: "By this will all people know that you are my disciples, if you have love for one another."[80] In John 21:5 which was added by a later redactor but within the johannine tradition, the disciples recognize Jesus in his final resurrection appearance when he addressed them as "children."[81]

According to the fourth gospel there were women among Jesus' own, his disciples. It is therefore possible that women were present when the disciples received the risen Jesus' solemn commission to ministry and the gift of his Holy Spirit:

> Peace be with you. As the Father has sent me, even so I send you. . . . Receive the Holy Spirit. If you forgive the sins of any, they are forgiven; if you retain the sins of any, they are retained.[82]

The fourth gospel placed the least emphasis on the Twelve among the gospels and the greatest emphasis upon discipleship. It is not surprising that it also gave women the most prominent role as disciples. The characters which appear in the fourth gospel are symbolic. Their number is fewer than those in the snyoptic gospels, but their role in instructing the johannine community in the faith of Christianity is much greater. That five major characters in the fourth gospel are women is in itself highly significant. That women were given the role played by Peter in the synoptics at the two most important moments in his movement from discipleship to apostleship, the confession of faith at Caesarea Philippi and the reception of the primary appearance and commission of the risen Jesus, points to the great importance of women both in johannine tradition and in the contemporary life of the johannine church. It is clear that for the fourth evangelist there were women disciples during the historical ministry of Jesus, just as there were women ministers in the Christian community where he lived and served. It raises the question whether some women may have actually been among the historical leaders of the johannine community. Raymond Brown summarized the portrait of discipleship in the fourth gospel: "A woman and a man stood at the foot of the Cross as models of Jesus' 'own,' his true family of disciples."[83]

Conclusion: The Discipleship of Women in the Four Gospels

Women disciples of Jesus are found in all four gospels. The shape and extent of the role of these women were qualified by each individual evangelist according to his own theological biases. Matthew tended to minimize the role of women from a rabbinic standpoint, whereas Luke did the same from a Greek standpoint. Matthew and Luke gave the most prominent position to the Twelve, all of whom were male, and the least important role to the women.[84] The fourth gospel, which gave the least amount of emphasis to the Twelve, gave the most prominent role to the women. The connection between these two different emphases may be significant. By the time the evangelists were writing most of the Twelve were already dead and the role of the Twelve as an institution in the Church had long ceased. Therefore the mention of the Twelve by an evangelist reflects his own theological preoccupations and ecclesial experience as much or more than it did the actual historical role of the Twelve during the lifetime of Jesus. Similarly the evangelists' portrait of women reflected their own time and theological attitudes. For this reason it is possible to find information about the ministerial roles of women in the churches in the latter half of the first century in the four evangelists' portrayal of the discipleship of women in the time of Jesus. In this area it would be especially useful to have more information concerning the provenance of the various gospel traditions. Hopefully in the future scholars will investigate more fully the social situations of the various Christian communities which produced these gospel traditions to establish in greater detail the position and role of women within these communities.

THE MINISTRIES OF WOMEN
IN THE EARLY CHURCH

Women Apostles

After the resurrection of Jesus many of his disciples who had remained faithful and had seen the risen Lord were henceforth called "apostles," which means "persons sent on a mission." In the pauline letters there were two criteria for apostleship: having seen the risen Jesus and having been commissioned by him.[85] The Lukan writings added a third criterion: having accompanied Jesus during his historical lifetime.[86]

The four gospels witness to the fulfillment of all three criteria by women. Women are not explicitly called "apostles" in the gospels, although they are in the pauline letters, but it must be kept in mind that "apostle" was a post-resurrection term and therefore not properly applicable to any characters in the gospels which conclude with the narrative of the resurrection.[87] The gospels do clearly show that women met all of the criteria which were later established by the early Church to determine who should be officially considered an apostle.

Even Luke, despite the restriction of the role of women in his writings, does attest to the fulfillment of his own third criterion by the women. He mentioned the presence of Mary of Magdala, Joanna and Susanna by name during the itinerant preaching ministry of Jesus. He also noted the presence of "many other" women.[88] It was these women and the Twelve whom Luke portrayed accompanying Jesus during his ministry. In the passion narrative, Luke again mentioned the presence of the women who had been with Jesus in Galilee, who faithfully continued to follow Jesus at the crucifixion.[89] The women disciples met Luke's criterion for apostleship, whereas Paul did not, since he had not accompanied Jesus during his lifetime.

The first pauline criterion of apostleship was that the person had seen the risen Jesus. The gospel resurrection narratives distinguish between the empty tomb stories and the resurrection appearances as such. All four gospels attest to the presence of women at the empty tomb. But this was secondary in importance to the actual witness of an appearance of the risen Jesus. The gospels of Matthew, John and the secondary ending of Mark attest that not only did the risen Jesus appear to women, but that he made his very first resurrection appearance to the women. Mary of Magdala is named in all three traditions. Matthew added another woman, also named Mary. Scripture scholars are in accord that the report of this initial appearance to one or more women must be historically accurate, since it would be utterly unlikely for an evangelist, writing within the misogynistic culture of the late first century, to have invented it.[90]

The second pauline criterion was the personal reception of a commission to ministry from the risen Jesus himself. The three gospels which describe an initial resurrection appearance to women include within the scene either an explicit commission to go and bear witness of the resurrection or ascension to the other disciples, or presuppose such a commission by noting that the women immediately did go and bear witness to the other disciples.[91] The gospels of Matthew, Luke and John also present the women bearing witness to the other disciples of the empty tomb.[92] Thus women are portrayed by the gospels as the first preachers of the good news of the resurrection of Jesus to the Christian community.

A further dimension of apostleship which was presupposed but not explicitly listed as a criterion was the reception of the Holy Spirit. According to Luke, the core group of the early Church, gathered in the upper room in Jerusalem awaiting the manifestation of the Spirit at Pentecost, consisted of three subgroups: the Eleven, who reconstituted their number to twelve in anticipation of Pentecost, the women witnesses of the resurrection appearances, and the mother and brothers of Jesus.[93]

The Pentecost account itself began with the note that they "were all together in one place." It is more reasonable to assume that this group included all those mentioned in the earlier verse than to suggest that, despite the use of the word "all," the women had somehow been excluded. A further confirmation of the presence of the women at Pentecost was the citation of the prophecy of Joel within the sermon of Peter. The text of such sermons is determined by the Lukan redactor. The Lukan framework of the entire Pentecost narrative is certainly male-oriented. Luke employed the word "men" seven times in the petrine speeches of Acts 1–2, a usage which had no possible Aramaic antecedent.[94] In the light of this generally restrictive Lukan attitude toward women, it is all the more remarkable that the Joel prophecy was chosen in this context. Joel had described the outpouring of the Spirit on men and women, "sons and daughters," "menservants and maidservants."[95]

The fact that Mary of Magdala was mentioned by name in all four resurrection narratives suggests that she was recognized as the leader among the group of women witnesses. Of all the women who appear in the gospels, the tradition of Mary of Magdala's apostleship is the strongest and most difficult to refute. There is no question that she was presented by the evangelists as meeting the two pauline and the additional Lukan criteria for apostleship.

The fourth gospel heightened the drama of the first scene of its

resurrection narrative through the contrast between the characters of
Mary of Magdala and Peter. Peter entered the empty tomb first, but
did not believe and went back home. Mary of Magdala then looked
into the tomb and saw the angels. The angels' address to Mary is repeated to her by Jesus. When he called her by name, she recognized
him and believed. According to johannine theology this doubly confirmed her discipleship: it portrayed her as one of Jesus' own and as
believing, both of which were essential for the true disciple. Then she
was given the apostolic commission by the risen Jesus.[96] She is portrayed in the following verse as fulfilling this mission by pronouncing
the standard formula of the apostolic proclamation of the resurrection: "I have seen the Lord."[97] Thus Mary of Magdala was the first
apostle.

According to Paul, primacy of witness to the risen Jesus, which
he personally attributed to Peter, was connected with primacy of authority within the apostolic Church. However both John and Matthew present independent traditions that a woman, Mary of
Magdala, held this primacy. In the early second century, when the
leadership role of women was retained only in the heterodox gnostic
churches, the final redactor of the fourth gospel added chapter 21 in
which Peter, who had been unfaithful to his discipleship through his
betrayal of Jesus, was rehabilitated as disciple and commissioned as
apostle to the pastoral care of the Church.[98]

The parallel roles of Mary of Magdala and Peter are found also
in early apochryphal literature. The gnostic gospel of Thomas, the
gospel according to Mary and the Pistis Sophia presented the leadership role of Mary of Magdala in the early Christian community as
equal to that of Peter.[98B] Later tradition called her the "apostle to the
apostles," affirming her role as sent by Jesus to bear witness to the
other disciples, thus bringing them also to faith in the resurrection.[99]

Thus there is a strong fourfold gospel tradition which presents
at least one woman, Mary of Magdala, as having fulfilled all the criteria of apostleship and as having exercised her apostleship at the
very least in her critically important mission to the other disciples.
Although her name predominates there are traditions of other wom-
en who also met the criteria of apostleship. Therefore it is evident
from the texts of the New Testament that there were women apostles

in the earliest days of the Christian Church. And it is no longer possible to argue that women cannot theologically serve in the ministry of the Church because all the apostles were men.[100]

There were also women missionary apostles, at least in the pauline churches. One woman, Junia, is explicitly called an "apostle" by Paul. In Romans 16:7 he referred to Andronicus and Junia, who had become Christian before him, as "outstanding among the apostles." Until the thirteenth century most commentators understood Junia as the name of a woman.[101] The feminine name is common in Greek.[102] In the thirteenth century a man, Aegidius of Rome, substituted the variant reading *"juliam"* which is also a feminine name, and pronounced this person to be a man *(vir)*. Other commentators followed suit. Martin Luther understood the name as "junias" which is masculine, but unattested in hellenistic Greek.[103] The influence of his position may be seen in the fact that most English translations today simply repeat this masculine form, Junias. Contemporary biblical scholars have attempted to give support to this interpretation by conjecturing that Junias was an abbreviation of a more common masculine name such as Junianus, Junianius or Junilius.[104] It is more prudent to follow the conservative commentator M.-J. Lagrange and retain the feminine Junia, which is the form which is in the New Testament text and which is attested as a common name in contemporary hellenistic Greek.[105]

On the evidence of the New Testament text and the interpretation of the early Fathers it is possible to assert that the apostle Junia was, in fact, a woman. Over the centuries male commentators have sought to obscure this fact, since it would threaten the presupposition that the official ministry of the Church was from the beginning reserved to men.

Junia herself was an official minister of great importance in the primitive diaspora church. Paul himself acknowledged and respected her authority. It is possible that she, like Paul, had personally founded churches, since this was the primary role of the missionary apostle. For Paul the authenticity of Christian apostleship was confirmed by two factors: fruitfulness and suffering.[106] Romans 16:7 explicitly affirms that Junia and Andronicus had suffered, and implies also that their apostolate had been fruitful.[107] It is possible that Junia and Andronicus were married to each other and like that other great

Christian pair Prisca and Aquila functioned as an apostolic mission-ary couple.[108]

Elsewhere in his letters Paul mentioned "apostles of the churches" who, like the Jewish *sheluhîm,* were official emissaries of the churches of Macedonia and Philippi.[109] Paul had high praise for such apostles as the "glory of Christ."[110] Elisabeth S. Fiorenza[111] has suggested that Phoebe, mentioned in Romans 16:1, may have exer-cised a similar role. Paul called her a *"diakonos."* Later in the cen-tury this word denoted the office of deacon. In this early period it may still have retained its more general meaning of "minister" while at the same time being in the process of developing in the direction of denoting an ecclesiastical office. According to Fiorenza Paul used the terms *"diakonos"* and *"apostolos"* interchangeably.[112] Paul spoke very highly of Phoebe. She was being sent as the official emissary of the church of Cenchraeae to the church of Rome. It was customary for Paul to give the apostles of the churches his official recommenda-tion, as he did for Phoebe in this passage.

Thus it has been demonstrated that there were women among both the Judean and the diaspora apostles in the early Church ac-cording to the evidence of the New Testament. The apostolate of the early Church was inclusive. It was not restricted only to men. The institution of the Twelve was, on the other hand, definitely restricted to men. But it has been shown above that the institutions of the apos-tolate and of the Twelve were not identical in the New Testament. The role of the Twelve was eschatological and symbolic, not ministe-rial.

The ministry of the Church was first embodied in the office of apostle, not in the institution of the Twelve. It was from the apostles that the functions of ministry were handed down. According to the evidence of the New Testament there were both men and women apostles in the primitive Church. There is no evidence in the New Testament writings on apostleship to support the exclusion of wom-en from the succession of apostolic ministry in the later Church.

Women Prophets

Paul listed prophecy second in importance after his own minis-try of apostleship in his lists of charismatic ministries in the Church.[113] In his theology of the charisms, Paul described prophecy as second only to love as most important among the gifts of the Holy Spirit.[114] Prophecy in the early Church was a ministry of word, of proclamation for the building up of the Christian community.[115] It was a charismatic ministry and one which was specifically ecclesial.[116] Prophecy was closely associated with teaching. It was also a liturgical ministry.[117] Prophets and teachers presided at eucharistic worship.[118] They were also recognized as leaders of the community. Prophets and teachers made official decisions and commissioned other Christians for special missions.[119]

Women functioned as prophets in the early Church. The daughters of Philip were recognized as prophetic leaders in spite of Luke's characteristic avoidance of portraying women as exercising any ministry of word.[120] Paul himself, in the context of a passage in which he was attempting to restrict the liturgical role of women in the church of Corinth, admitted that women had the right to function as prophets in the Christian assembly.[121] There is also mention of a woman in Revelation 2:20 who was a leader of the church of Thyatira.[122] It is stated that she was called prophet and that she taught, although her teaching had deviated from orthodoxy.

Thus in the first century Church women were accepted as prophets. As such they would have exercised a role of proclamation of the word and presidence at liturgical celebrations. The functions of the office of prophet were absorbed by the office of bishop in the second century. Those prophets who remained independent found themselves outside the domain of orthodoxy which was controlled by the bishop. As heresies were suppressed, in many of which women prophets had played an important role,[123] and as the office of bishop became more powerful, the office of prophet disappeared from the Church. Yet through the ages, men and women have exercised a prophetic ministry within the Church, although without official approbation or recognized office. Many such men and women eventually came to be called saints.

Women Presiders at Eucharistic Worship

The early history of eucharistic worship in the Church has remained clouded in obscurity. The New Testament recounts the story of the last supper in the gospel passion narratives. The synoptic gospels present the account of the blessing and sharing of the bread and cup by Jesus which tradition has called the "institution of the eucharist." The synoptic narratives do not, with the exception of a disputed verse in Luke added by a later editor,[124] include the injunction to "do this in memory of me." This command is found for certain only in the pauline version of the institution narrative in 1 Corinthians 11:23–25. The latter passage is an early pre-pauline liturgical formula which was used in eucharistic worship in the Church before the time of Paul's writing. Since at that time the eucharist had become a rite of the Church, the injunction to continue the practice of the rite had become an essential part of the liturgy. The gospels, although written later, did not include it in the last supper narratives. In the synoptic accounts Jesus was portrayed as sharing his body and blood with his disciples as a symbol of the new covenant which would the next day be sealed by his death on the cross. The fourth gospel mentioned the supper[125] but omitted the institution narrative altogether.

Who was present at the last supper? It is not possible to know the precise names of all who were present. But it is significant to note that all four gospels mention the presence of the "disciples," a general term which included many more persons than just the Twelve, and which included some women.[126] In the preceding and subsequent scenes of the preparation for the meal and Gethsemane the persons accompanying Jesus are uniformly called the "disciples."[127] It is only in the pericopes concerning Judas that the Twelve are mentioned.[128] This is the only mention of the Twelve in the entire Passion Narrative. It may have been embedded in a special Judas source or have been retained as a relevant detail noting that Judas was a member of the Twelve. Thus the evidence indicates that a greater number of disciples than just the Twelve were present at the last supper. The fourth gospel described those present as Jesus' "own," a term which, as was demonstrated above, denoted the disciples and included at least one woman, Mary of Magdala.

The last supper narratives in Mark, Matthew and John are immediately preceded by the account of the anointing of Jesus by a woman at Bethany. The conjunction of the two narratives suggests that they were connected in the tradition. The faith, generosity and understanding of the woman stood in stark contrast to the deceit and betrayal of Judas. The two stories were actually interwoven in John 12:4–6. The woman was presented as the true disciple of Jesus. Judas, though one of the Twelve, was shown to be a false disciple.

In the Markan and Matthean accounts the woman anointed the head of Jesus as a sign of his messianic identity. The johannine scene is even more dramatic. There[129] Mary of Bethany anointed the feet of Jesus and wiped them with her hair. In the following chapter the johannine version of the last supper omitted the institution narrative and substituted the scene of Jesus washing the feet of his disciples and wiping them with a piece of his own clothing. There it was explicitly stated that the disciples were commanded to do as Jesus did.[130] Then Jesus taught the disciples that the true nature of his identity is that of servant.[131] As Jesus their Lord was a servant and washed their feet, so therefore his true disciples would likewise be servants and wash each other's feet, as Mary of Bethany had just done.

Thus the gospel accounts of the last supper do not contain any commission to ministry as such except the command in John to be servants as Jesus was servant. There is no question of "ordination" in the last supper scenes. This interpretation was read back into scripture by later sacramental theologians. The solemn commission to ministry in the gospels was given after the resurrection, because it was dependent upon faith in the risen Jesus. It was confirmed and empowered through the event of Pentecost, the moment at which the Church was born.[132]

Within a decade or two of the resurrection some form of the practice of eucharistic worship did exist in the Church. That it was known to and practiced by Paul is evident from his recounting the institution formula in 1 Corinthians 11:23–25. Acts 27:35 may describe a scene in which Paul presided at a eucharistic celebration on a ship at sea. These texts suggest that presiding at eucharistic worship could be a function of an apostle. Acts 13:1–2 mentions prophets and teachers as the leaders of worship. That prophets and teachers, were the ordinary ministers of the eucharist, is confirmed by the *Didache*.[133] By the turn of the second century this function began to pass to the bishops and deacons.[134] In the New Testament period as such the only definite references to presiders at eucharistic worship are to missionary apostles, prophets and teachers. There were women missionary apostles and women prophets. There were most likely also women teachers.[135] Thus it is quite possible that women were among the first Christian ministers of the eucharist. There is no evidence to exclude the possibility of women presiding at eucharistic worship until the close of the New Testament period.[136]

Women Fellow Workers

In many of his letters Paul wrote of other ministers of the gospel whom he called "fellow workers." It is doubtful whether this title referred to any specific office in the Church. It designated those who, like Paul, served the Christian community through ministry. Paul called such persons both "my fellow workers" and "our fellow workers" and also "God's fellow workers."[137] There were women among those whom he addressed as his own fellow workers: Prisca, Euodia and Syntyche.[138] There were also men: Aquila, Timothy, Mark, Aristarchus, Demas, Luke, Epaphroditus and Justus.[139] Those addressed as "our fellow workers" were men: Urbanus, Philemon and Titus. Those named as God's fellow workers were also men: Apollos, Paul himself, and possibly also Timothy.

There is no evidence for distinguishing different types of fellow workers.[140] The use of the term "God's" fellow worker in 1 Corinthians was probably necessitated by Paul's inclusion of himself. It would have been redundant to use his more usual designation of "my" or "our" when referring to himself. If the variant reading of 1 Thessalonians 3:2 is accepted, then Timothy would be called both "God's" and "my" fellow worker Although women were explicitly named only as "my" fellow workers, it must be noted that one of "God's" fellow workers, Apollos, had himself been instructed by a woman.[141]

The term "fellow worker" (synergos) in the pauline letters may not designate an ecclesiastical office. It is questionable whether at this time formal offices yet existed in the Church. But it did denote persons who were prominent in the ministry of the pauline churches. Whenever the term was used by Paul, he named those who were his fellow workers by name, expecting his readers to know who they were.

Paul's own primary category for understanding his own ministry was apostleship. By this he meant bearing authentic witness to the gospel of Jesus through proclamation and suffering. It is possible that Paul intended to associate those whom he called "fellow workers" with his own ministry of apostleship. Certainly there is evidence that at least some of the persons called fellow workers, Timothy, Titus, Prisca and Aquila, accompanied Paul in his itinerant ministry as missionary apostle.

The important point was that the fellow workers shared with Paul in the ministry of the Church, the ministry of service to the churches. What precise forms or categories shaped their understanding of ministry in this early period are not known, probably because they were still in the stage of flexibility and development. The fellow workers of Paul did, however, possess authority.[142] Whatever the ministry of the apostolic fellow worker actually was, there is solid evidence in the New Testament that this ministry was exercised by both women and men.[143]

Women Preachers and Evangelists

At least one, if not the primary, function of the fellow workers of Paul was evangelization and proclamation of the gospel. The women Euodia and Syntyche worked side by side with Paul "in the gospel."[144] Prisca, another fellow worker, instructed Apollos in the correct doctrine for preaching.[145] These women participated in the work of evangelization alongside their brothers.[146]

In the letter to the Romans,[147] Paul named four women, Mary, Tryphaena, Tryphosa and Persis, all of whom he called "hard workers" in the Lord. The usage of the verb *kopian* ("to work hard") in the pauline letters approached a technical denotation of preaching and evangelism.[148] Paul frequently associated this verb with his own work of preaching and evangelism.[149] Later on the pastoral epistles described presbyters as "hard workers in preaching and teaching."[150] Paul himself acknowledged "hard working" as a ministry of leadership which commanded authority in the Christian community. In 1 Corinthians 16:16 Paul urged the Christians of Corinth to be subject to those in the ministry of service and to the "hard workers and fellow workers." In 1 Thessalonians 5:12 Paul encouraged the showing of respect, esteem and love to the "hard workers."

Whether "hard working" was ever a formal office in the Church is not known for certain. Yet it did designate a form of ministry in the time of Paul and this ministry involved the functions of preaching and evangelization. This ministry was definitely exercised by women, four of whom were prominent enough to have been mentioned by name in Romans.

By the end of the first century, the pastoral epistles seem to indicate that the ministry of preaching and teaching was in the process of being absorbed by the office of presbyter.[151] As the first century office of presbyter merged with the office of bishop, and as the latter was in subsequent centuries reinterpreted through the Old Testament model of levitical high priesthood, women come to be excluded from both offices and from the function of preaching in the Church, a ministry which they had been free to exercise during the New Testament period at least in the pauline churches.

Women Deacons

The diaconate developed gradually into an ecclesiastical office. In the earliest Church the term *diakonia* denoted Christian ministry in general. Later it came to denote a specific ministry in the Church. But it was only in the second century, after the establishment of the monarchical episcopacy, that it came to mean a hierarchical office, subordinate to the office of bishop. The direction of this development is foreshadowed in the pastoral epistles at the close of the New Testament period, but the full development of a hierarchy of office was post-biblical.

In the gospels it is frequently mentioned that women "served" (*diakonein*).[152] Jesus is portrayed as accepting and affirming their ministry of service. In the synoptic gospels women are shown primarily serving Jesus himself. Only these women remained faithful to their service at the crucifixion and burial of Jesus. Then it was these same ministering women who were chosen to be the witnesses of Jesus' first resurrection appearance and who were commissioned to continue their ministry by bearing witness of the resurrection to other disciples.

As the diaconate developed into an office in the Church, the New Testament indicates that women did serve as deacons. In Romans 16:1 it is stated that Phoebe was a deacon of the church of Cenchraeae. The Greek word *diakos* is used, which is masculine, not the feminine form *diakonissa,* which was used in patristic literature to denote the later office of deaconess. Paul commended Phoebe to the church of Rome to which she was being sent as an official messenger. Paul acknowledged that she had been "a helper of many and of myself as well."[153] On the basis of the text of Romans 16:1 it is possible to affirm that insofar as the office of deacon had developed in the Church at this time, it was exercised by women as well as men.

Toward the end of the first century, there appeared in 1 Timothy 3:8–13 the most detailed passage in the New Testament on the office of deacon. Verse 11 listed the qualifications for women. In the past commentators often explained this away by saying that women were merely the wives of deacons,[154] or else that they were only admitted to the inferior office of deaconess. However there is no evidence in the text of 1 Timothy to support either of the above interpretations. The office of deaconess appeared only later, in the patristic period, when women were being excluded from official ministry in the Church. A simpler and more conservative understanding of 1 Timothy 3:11 is that there were, in fact, women deacons in the Church in the first century.[155] Both women and men exercised the same office of deacon, and on an equal basis. This interpretation is supported by a reference in a letter of Pliny the Younger, written around the beginning of the second century, to Christian women who served and who were called ministers or deacons.[156]

Raymond Brown has suggested[157] that the reference in John 12:2 to the service of Martha may reflect the time and church order of the evangelist who was writing in the 90's when the office of deacon had been officially established in the Church and was exercised by women in his community. Luke 10:40 also associated the word *diakonia* with the ministry of Martha. If this hypothesis is correct, it could apply to other references to women "serving" in the gospels, such as Peter's mother-in-law, and Mary of Magdala and the women disciples from Galilee.[158] It may, however, refer to the general ministry of these women. Whether the use of *diakonein* in the gospels connoted diaconal or apostolic ministy is impossible to decide without further evidence.

The New Testament information about the diaconate as an office, its establishment and its functions, is minimal. The texts which do make explicit reference to it indicate that both men and women served as deacons in the early Church, especially in the pauline churches.

The radical equality of the sexes in Christ was theologically underscored by Paul in the baptismal catechesis of Galatians 3:28. Yet such an official public role for women was contrary to social custom in contemporary Judaism and in Graeco-Roman society. It is probable that the pressure of the mores of the contemporary cultural milieu contributed to the early demise of the practice of women exercising the office of deacon in the Church and the substitution of the inferior, but socially more acceptable, office of deaconess. The ministry of the deaconess was generally limited to women. She was not permitted to serve the Christian community as a whole. It is also possible that the introduction of the exclusively male office of the levitical priest as a model for Christian ministry in the second century and the subsequent eclipse of the office of deacon by that of priest were also causal factors in the exclusion of women from the ecclesiastical office of deacon which they had been free to exercise in the New Testament period.[159]

Women as Apostolic Wives: Married Ministry in the Early Church

In general attitudes which are positive or negative toward the position and role of women in church and society are also often correspondingly positive or negative concerning the value of marriage. In the New Testament Christian thinkers began to grapple with the question of the value of marriage. In Judaism marriage had been the norm, enjoined by law upon every righteous Jewish man. Marriage also continued to be the norm for most Christians during the first century, especially for those exercising official ministries in the Church.

Two important figures in the early history of ministry in the Church were Prisca and Aquila. They were mentioned in Acts, in two of the major pauline letters and in the pastoral epistles. Although the latter were written much later in time, the ministry of the couple was still remembered in the Church.[160]

Prisca and Aquila were Paul's fellow workers in Christ.[161] They had proved the authenticity of their ministry through suffering persecution.[162] They were the recognized leaders of the church which met in their house.[163]

Like Paul they were tentmakers by profession, and they used their trade to support themselves and other Christians.[164] Yet they were not bound to house or job. They exercised the freedom of apostolic missionaries, accompanying Paul on journeys and traveling to minister to other Christian communities.[165]

Prisca and Aquila were not uneducated. They exercised a ministry of the word for which they had been trained. Even Apollos, who was himself described as "eloquent," "well versed in the scriptures," "instructed in the way," and who spoke and taught well about Christianity, even to being accepted as a preacher in the synagogue, was corrected and reinstructed by Prisca and Aquila whose theological learning was greater and more accurate.[166] The New Testament bears witness that a women, Prisca, ministered to the man, Apollos.

Junia and Andronicus are also mentioned as a couple. Within contemporary social mores this would be unlikely unless they were either married to each other, or brother and sister.[167] They too had proved the authenticity of their ministry through suffering for the Lord. Paul addressed them with respect, calling them "outstanding among the apostles." All that is known of their ministry is that they were apostles, which involved proclamation of the word, and that they suffered.

Many of the apostles were married and were accompanied by their wives in this apostolic ministry. According to Paul this was the custom. "Do we not have the right to be accompanied by a wife, as the other apostles and the brothers of the Lord and Cephas?"[168] Thus in the diaspora churches in the middle of the first century, married ministry was the norm. Celibacy was an exception which required justification.[169] Thus it is possible that the women also exercised a shared ministry with their husbands in their role as apostolic wives.

The New Testament explicitly states that the apostles, bishops and deacons of the early Church were, as a rule, married.[170] It did not make either marriage or celibacy a condition for holding ecclesiastical office. It did, however, emphasize the importance of moral character within marriage and in all areas of life, as well as faith, knowledge of sound doctrine and the ability to teach it to the people, as important qualities for those in ministry.[171]

Conclusion

In the New Testament there were not ministries of men and ministries of women. There were only ministries of Jesus in which both men and women served. Jesus himself ministered to God's people as servant. He called his followers to do the same.

The form of ministry which is most authentically Christian is that which is most totally conformed to the nature of Jesus' own ministry. The ministry of Jesus was that of service, service to all human persons, regardless of class, sex or merit, service of atoning, self-offering love. In general Christian ministry in the New Testament is portrayed as ministry of service. Apostles, prophets, teachers, evangelists, pastors and deacons—all served the people of God, each with his or her own gifts, for the building up of the Christian community in love.

There is nothing inherent in the character of Christian ministry as it is presented in the writings of the New Testament which would give reason for the exclusion of women. On the contrary, the New Testament portrays Jesus treating women as equal human persons. It also portrays women and men serving side by side in the various ministries of the early Church.

The later exclusion of women from the official ministry of the Church raises serious questions about the authenticity of such a practice. According to the evidence of the New Testament, the exclusion of women from ecclesiastical ministry is neither in accord with the teaching or practice of Jesus nor with that of the first century Church.

The New Testament presents the call of Jesus as universally inclusive. Both the call of Jesus to discipleship and the call to ministerial service in the early Church were universal. They were not restricted by sex, marital status, social class, race or nationality. Authentic Christian ministry in the Church ought to be conformed to the norm of sacred scripture and to its teaching about the nature of ministry.

NOTES

1. Mk 8:34.
2. Mt 23:8–12.
3. Mk 1:16–20, 2:13–14.
4. Cf. Mk 9:35, 10:43, 45, 15:41.
5. Vincent Taylor, *The Gospel According to St. Mark* (London: Macmillan, 1966), p. 178.
6. A variant reading added "sisters" in the first part of the verse, which strengthens the case that "sisters" in the second part is genuine. The editor would have been attempting to make the first part an exact parallel to the second.
7. M.-J. Lagrange, *Évangile selon saint Marc* (Paris: Gabalda, 1929), p. 78.
8. K. L. Schmidt, *Der Rahmen der Geschichte Jesu* (Berlin: Trowitzsch, 1919), p. 154.
9. Mk 5:24–34.
10. Taylor, *op. cit.*, p. 347.
11. The omission of "fathers" may reflect Jesus' prohibition in Mt 23:9 against calling anyone "father" except God.
12. Cf. Mk 10:17–25.
13. 1 Sm 10:1, 2 Sm 5:3, 1 Kg 1:34, 39, 45.
14. Mk 16:9–11 shows the disciples refusing to believe Mary's witness, possibly because she was a woman, or possibly because throughout this gospel they have been portrayed as slow to understand and believe.
15. Mt 19:29.
16. Mt 26:6–13.
17. Mt 27:55–56.
18. "My brethren." Mt 28:9–10.
19. Mt 10:1, 11:1, 19:28, 28:16. All but the first are not paralleled in the other synoptic gospels.
20. Hans Conzelmann, *The Theology of St. Luke* (New York: Harper & Row, 1961), pp. 16–17. Cf. Lk 16:16.
21. This is the position of Elisabeth S. Fiorenza, unpublished address to the General Meeting of the Catholic Biblical Association of America, San Francisco, August 24, 1978.
22. Lk 1:45. cf. R. E. Brown, K. P. Donfried, J. A. Fitzmyer, J. Reumann, *Mary in the New Testament* (Philadelphia/New York: Fortress/Paulist, 1978), 136.
23. Brown, *et.al.*, *Mary*, 142 interpret this scene as presenting Mary proclaiming the gospel "by anticipation." It must be kept in mind, however, that for Luke this is still the faith of Israel.
24. 1 Tm 5:9, 11, 14 (age and marital status), 5:5 (prayer), 5:10 (service). Raymond E. Brown, *The Birth of the Messiah* (Garden City, N. Y.: Doubleday, 1977), p. 467.

25. Conzelmann, *op. cit.,* 215. Brown, *et al., Mary,* 126, 143, 163 find a continuity in the discipleship of Mary through the her faith and through a connection with the theme of God's poor (the *anawîm).* It should be noted that even if Luke presented her as a disciple in the periods of Israel and Jesus, she is not mentioned in the period of the Church.

26. Lk 8:2–3.

27. Brown, "Roles," p. 697. Brown, *et. al., Mary,* 168.

28. Brown, *et. al., Mary,* 172.

29. Lk 7:36–50.

30. Walter Bauer (William F. Arndt and F. Wilbur Gingrich, eds.), *A Greek-English Dictionary of the New Testament and Other Early Christian Literature* (Cambridge: Cambridge University Press, 1957), p. 791.

31. Lk 24:22–24, 34.

32. Lk 24:47–48.

33. Constance F. Parvey, "The Theology and Leadership of Women in the New Testament," in Rosemary R. Ruether (ed.), *Religion and Sexism* (New York: Simon & Schuster, 1974), pp. 139–140. E. S. Fiorenza, CBA Address.

34. Ac 5:14, 8:3, 12, 9:2, 17:12, 22:4.

35. Ac 1:14. Most scholars assume that they remained together through the Pentecost event. Cf. Brown, *et al., Mary,* 176–177.

36. Ac 2:17–18, Joel 2:28–32.

37. Brown, *et. al., Mary.,* 175, 284.

38. Ac 2:22, 29, 3:12, 17, 13:16, 26.

39. Ac 7:2.

40. Believing: the mother of Timothy in Ac 16:1, Damaris in Ac 17:34. Praying: Ac 21: 5. Objects of healings: Ac 9:36–40.

41. Ac 12:12–17.

42. Ac 5:1–11.

43. Ac 13:50.

44. Ac 24:24, 25:13, 23, 26:30.

45. Ac 12:12, 16:15, 40.

46. Ac 21:9.

46B. 1 Cor 16:19, Rm 16:3. Cf. 2 Tm 4:19.

47. Ac 18:1–3, 18–19.

47B. The word was used of Mary of Magdala in the Gospel of Peter 12:50.

48. Haenchen, *op. cit.,* p. 341.

49. Fiorenza, CBA Address.

50. Cf. Brown, *John* I, xli–li.

51. Jn 2–12.

52. This is in accord with the synoptic gospels, which also portray Mary as playing no role as Jesus' mother in his ministry. Cf. Brown, "Roles," p. 697. Cf. Mk 3:31–35 pars.

53. Jn 19:25–27.

54. Brown, "Roles," pp. 698–699.
55. *Ibid.,* p. 691.
56. Jn 4:25–26, 29.
57. Jn 4:28–29.
58. Jn 4:39.
59. Jn 17:20 (RSV).
60. Jn 4:38–39. Brown, "Roles," pp. 691–692.
61. Brown, *John* I, 173.
62. Jn 11:25–26.
63. Brown, "Roles," p. 693. Especially Mt 16:16, the climactic midpoint of Mt.
64. Jn 1:49, 20:31 Cf. Jn 1:20.
65. Jn 11:3.
66. Jn 11:1. Brown, "Roles," p. 694, n. 19.
67. Brown, "Roles," p. 690.
68. Brown, *John* I, 447.
69. Jn 19:25.
70. Brown, *John,* II, 984 notes the possibility that the plural "we" in this verse might denote a trace of the presence of others in his source.
71. Jn 20:2. However, at this point Mary of Magdala did not understand the significance of the empty tomb or believe in the resurrection.
72. Jn 20:11–18.
73. Jn 10:14 (RSV).
74. Cf. Jn 13: 1.
75. Jn 20:16.
76. Jn 10:3.
77. Jn 16:19–22.
78. Jn 13:1, 33.
79. Bauer, *op. cit.,* p. 815.
80. Jn 13:35 (RSV). Cf. 1 Jn 3:10, 4:4, 7–8, 11–12. 1 Jn connects the two concepts.
81. The Greek word here is, however, *paidia.* This is also neuter and denotes children of both sexes. Cf. Bauer, *op. cit.,* p. 609, Brown, *John* II, 1070. In 1 Jn 2:12–14 the two are interchangeable and distinct from *neaniskos* which means "young man." In the vocabulary of the late first century the word *teknon* could denote a disciple or spiritual child, as in 1 Tm 1:2, 18, 2 Tm 1:2.
82. Jn 20:21–22 (RSV).
83. Brown, "Roles," p. 699.
84. Lk used the term "apostles" to denote the Twelve.
85. 1 Cor 15:3–9, Gal 1:11–17.
86. Ac 1:21.
87. The word "apostle" appears anachronistically in the gospels. Cf. Mk 6:30, Mt. 10:2, Lk 6:13, 9:10, 11:49, 17:5, 22:14, 24:10. Note that it appears most frequently in Lk. Lk used the term to denote the Twelve. This us-

age derived from a later stage of tradition and was influenced by the theology of the redactor. Cf. Fiorenza, "Twelve," p. 115.

88. Lk 8:1–3.

89. Lk 23:49, 55.

90. Mk 16:9–11, Mt 28:9–10, Lk 24:10, Jn 20:11–18. Cf. standard commentaries on these passages.

91. Jn 20:17, Mt 28:10, Mk 16:10.

92. Mt 28:8, Lk 24:10, Jn 20:2.

93. Ac 1:14. Cf. Fiorenza, "Apostleship," p. 136.

94. F. F. Bruce, *The Acts of the Apostles* (Grand Rapids: Eerdmans, 1968), p. 76. Bruce also cites G. M. Dalman, *Jesus-Jeshua* (New York: Ktav, 1971, reprint of 1929 ed.), p. 22.

95. Ac 2:17–18, Joel 2:28–32.

96. Jn 20:17.

97. Jn 20:18 (RSV). Brown, "Roles," p. 692.

98. 1 Cor 15:2–9, Mt 28:9–10, Jn 20:11–18. Raymond E. Brown, *The Community of the Beloved Disciple* (New York: Paulist, 1979), 161–162, 189.

98B. Fiorenza, "Apostleship," p. 140, n. 6.

99. Rabanus Maurus, PL 112, 1474b (cited by Brown, "Roles," p. 693, n. 14), Bernard of Clairvaux, *Sermones in Cant.* 75, 8, PL 183, 1148 (cited by E. S. Fiorenza, "Feminist Theology as a Critical Theology of Liberation," *Theological Studies* 36 (1975), p. 625), Hippolytus, *Comm. in Cant.* (cited by Jean Daniélou, *The Ministry of Women in the Early Church* (London: Faith Press, 1961), p. 16).

100. The 1976 Vatican Declaration maintained that the practice of Jesus and the apostles was normative for the Church today (18). However, it then went on to interpret this practice in terms of the exclusion of women from the apostolate in the first century (19). It based this assumption more upon ecclesiastical tradition than upon critical biblical scholarship. Such methodology would be contrary to the teaching of *Divino afflante Spiritu* (the encyclical of Pius XII, issued in 1943, which encouraged the critical study of the Bible by Catholic scholars).

101. Bernadette Brooten, " 'Junia . . . Outstanding Among the Apostles (Romans 16:7),' " in Swidler, *Women Priests,* p. 141. She cites Origen, Chrysostom, Jerome, Hatto, Theophylact, and Abelard.

102. For example, a first century A. D. inscription (cited in Lefkowitz-Fant, *op. cit.,* 113; Corinth, A.D. 43): "The deme of Patareia has decreed: Whereas Junia Theodora, a Roman resident in Corinth, a woman held in highest honor . . . who copiously supplied from her own means many of our citizens with generosity, and received them in her home and in particular never ceased acting on behalf of our citizens in regard to any favor asked— the majority of citizens have gathered in assembly to offer testimony on her behalf. Our people in gratitude agreed to vote: to commend Junia and to offer testimony of her generosity to our native city and of her good will, to testify that she increased her good will toward the city, because she knew that

our people also would not cease in their good will and gratitude toward her and would do everything for the excellence and the glory she deserved. For this reason (with good fortune), it was decreed to commend her for all that she had done." There is no reason to connect this Junia with the one mentioned in Rm.

103. Brooten, *art. cit.*, p. 142, cites M.-J. Lagrange, *Épître aux Romains* (Paris: Gabalda, ⁶1950), p. 366.

104. Brooten, *art. cit.*, p. 142.

105. Lagrange, *Romains,* p. 366.

106. 1 Cor 4:8–13, 2 Cor 11–12. Cf. 1 Cor 9:15–18.

107. Fiorenza, "Apostleship," p. 135.

108. Lagrange, *Romains,* p. 366. Cited by Elisabeth S. Fiorenza, "Women Apostles: The Testament of Scripture," A. M. Gardiner (ed.), *Women and Catholic Priesthood: An Expanded Vision* (New York: Paulist, 1976), pp. 96, 101, n.9.

109. 2 Cor 8:23 (Macedonia), Phl 2:25 (Philippi).

110. 2 Cor 8:23.

111. Fiorenza, "Apostleship," p. 137.

112. 2 Cor 11:13–15.

113. 1 Cor 12:28, Rm 12:6, Eph 4:11.

114. 1 Cor 14:1. Cf. 1 Cor 13:2.

115. 1 Cor 14:3.

116. 1 Cor 14:4.

117. Ac 13:1–2, Did 10:7, 15:1–2.

118. Did 15:1–2, Ac 13:1–2.

119. Ac 13:3.

120. Ac 21:9.

121. 1 Cor 11:5.

122. G. B. Caird, *A Commentary of the Revelation of St. John the Divine* (New York: Harper & Row, 1966), p. 43.

123. For example, in Montanism. Cf. G. Friedrich, *TDNT* VI, pp. 860–861 for references.

124. Lk 22:19b. Cf. Carroll Stuhlmueller, *JBC* II, p. 157, for comment on the textual problem.

125. Jn 13:2.

126. Mk 14:12, 13, 14, 16, 32, Mt 26:1, 17, 18, 19, 26, 35, 36, Lk 22:11, 39, Jn 13:5, 22, 23, 35, 18:1.

127. Lk used the term "apostles" in 22:14.

128. Mk 14:10 pars., 14:17 par., 14:20.

129. Jn 12:3.

130. Jn 13:14–15.

131. Jn 13:16.

132. In one sense ministerial office as such did not exist before Pentecost insofar as before that time the Church as such also did not exist.

133. Did 10:7, 15:1–2.

134. Did 15:1–2, Ignatius of Antioch, *Smryn* VIII 1–2. Cf. *Phil* IV 1.

135. Prisca was reported to have taught the missionary apostle Apollos. Cf. Ac 18:26.

136. 1 Cor 14:34–35 is considered an interpolation by a later editor, perhaps coming out of the same school which produced the pastoral epistles. Roger Gryson, *The Ministry of Women in the Early Church* (Collegeville: Liturgical Press, 1976), pp. 6–7, lists the various bases for this understanding: the variant position of the verses in some MSS, the broken continuity between vv. 33 and 36, unpauline vocabulary and syntax in the vv., content on the role of women which contradicts the views expressed elsewhere by Paul. Cf. C. K. Barrett, *A Commentary of the First Epistle to the Corinthians* (New York: Harper & Row, 1968), p. 330, Johannes Weiss, *Der erste Korintherbrief* (Göttingen: Vanderhoeck & Ruprecht, ⁹1910). Meeks, *art. cit.,* p. 201, states that "Paul nowhere denies women the right to engage in charismatic leadership of worship."

137. Rm 16:9, 21, Phm 24, Phl 2:25, 4:3, Col 4:11 ("my fellow workers"), Rm 16:9, Phm 1, Cf. 2 Cor 8:23 ("our fellow workers"), 1 Cor 3:9, variant reading of 1 Th 3:2 ("God's fellow workers").

138. Prisca in Rm 16:3, Euodia and Syntyche in Phl 4:3.

139. Aquila in Rm 16:3, Timothy in Rm 16:21, Mark, Aristarchus, Demas and Luke in Phlm 24, Epaphroditus in Phl 2:25, Aristarchus, Mark and Justus in Col 4:10–11.

140. Cf. Mary Ann Getty, "God's Fellow Worker and Apostleship," in Swidler, *Women Priests,* pp. 176–182. The reason why this point is being made is that the 1976 Vatican Declaration (17) made a distinction between the two types of fellow workers and said that "my" fellow workers informally helped Paul, while "God's" fellow workers designated those in official apostolic ministry. This distinction was used to confirm the assumption that women did not serve in apostolic ministry. There is little ground in the text of scripture or in current biblical scholarship to defend such a distinction.

141. Ac 18:26.

142. Cf. 1 Cor 16:16.

143. Cf. Rm 16:3, Phl 4:3, Getty, *art. cit.,* Vatican Declaration 16.

144. Phil 4:2–3.

145. Ac 18:26.

146. Daniélou, *op. cit.,* p. 8, Gryson, *op. cit.,* p. 5. Ignatius, *Phil* V, 2, indicates that prophets had the function of preaching. Thus it is possible that the women prophets also exercised the function of preaching.

147. Rm 16:6, 12.

148. Gryson, *op. cit.,* p. 5, states that *kopian* denotes evangelization. Daniélou, *op. cit.,* p. 8 uses it of evangelization and apostolic ministry. Meeks, *art. cit.,* p. 198, understood it as "teaching." In some instances Paul used this verb for his own work of tentmaking (1 Cor 4:12, 1 Th 2:9). This does not preclude the technical theological usage of the verb elsewhere.

149. 1 Cor 15:10–11, Gal 4:11, Phl 2:16, Col 1:28–29. Cf. 2 Cor 10:15–16.

150. 1 Tm 5:17.

151. 1 Tm 5:17.

152. Mk 1:31 pars. (Peter's mother-in-law), Lk 10:40 (Martha), Jn 12:2 (Martha), Mk 15:41 par. (the women at the cross).

153. Rm 16:2 (RSV). *Prostatis* denotes many different forms of active service, not merely financial support. Cf. Oepke, *TDNT* I, p. 787, as opposed to Gryson, *op. cit.,* p. 4.

154. The primary meaning of the word *gyne* in hellenistic Greek was "woman" (not "wife").

155. Lemaire, *art. cit.,* p. 45; Gryson, *op. cit.,* p. 8 states that their official function in the Church was analogous to that of the male deacons.

156. Pliny the Younger, *Epistle* 96. In the Latin text the "women who served" were called *ancillae,* and they were named *ministrae,* which is equivalent to the Greek *diakonoi.* The passage is cited by Daniélou, *op. cit.,* p. 15 and Oepke, *TDNT* I, p. 789.

157. Brown, "Roles," p. 690. He notes that Martha made the fourth gospel equivalent of the synoptic petrine confession (Mt 16:16 pars.) in Jn 11:27.

158. Mk 1:31 pars., 15:41 par., Mt 27:55. Cf. Lk 8:3.

159. The development began with 1 Clem 40–44 and Ignatius of Antioch, *Eph* IV, 1, *Magn* III, 1–2, VII, 1–2, *Trall* II, 1–3, III, 1–2, VII, 2, *Smyrn* VIII, 1–2, IX, 1.

160. 2 Tm 4:19.

161. Rm 16:3.

162. Rm 16:4.

163. Rm 16:5.

164. Ac 18:3.

165. Ac 18:18–19.

166. Ac 18:24–26. Meeks, *art. cit.,* p. 198, conjectures that the couple may have presided over catechetical schools in Ephesus, Corinth and Rome.

167. Rm 16:7. Lagrange, *Romains,* p. 366. assumed that they were married.

168. 1 Cor 9:5 (RSV)

169. 1 Cor 7:25–35.

170. 1 Cor 9:5 (apostles), 1 Tm 3:6 (bishops), 3:12 (deacons).

171. 1 Tm 3:2–13.

CONCLUSION

Jesus called both women and men to service in his Church. The earliest Christian communities followed the practice of Jesus. In the first century women exercised the ministries of disciple, apostle, prophet, deacon, proclaimer of the gospel and leader of worship. Despite the fact that women were not equal and were generally subordinate to men in contemporary Jewish, Hellenistic and Roman society, both Jesus and the early Church allowed women to hold and exercise ministerial office.

The New Testament gives an indication of many factors which were considered important conditions for Christian ministry, such as faith in the risen Jesus, commission by Jesus or by recognized ecclesiastical authorities, understanding of and ability to communicate the gospel message, and gifting by the Holy Spirit. But the sex of the minister was not relevant for ministerial office either in the teaching and practice of Jesus or in the earliest theology and exercise of ministry in the Church. Sex became a problem, beginning in the second half of the first century, when the Church began to come into conflict with its social milieu and began to adapt its own practice to the mores of that milieu.

In the same way the marital status of the disciple or minister was also irrelevant for the exercise of ministry in the New Testament era. The presence of a wife in the company of a male minister was considered normal, not as contaminating the minister. Those apostles, bishops and other ministers in the early Church who were not married were considered exceptional. Shared ministry exercised by husband and wife teams was a common phenomenon in the first century Church.

The primary model of ministry in the New Testament is service.

140   CONCLUSION

The ministry of Jesus was characterized through the application of the image and theology of the suffering servant. The gospels portrayed Jesus as teaching his disciples that the nature of their ministry was to be like his own, one of service. The Christian servant was to serve both God and the people through total self-offering even to death.

The Old Testament ministerial model of levitical priesthood is absent from the pages of the New Testament. It is mentioned only in passing reference to contemporary Jewish priest, but its application to Christian ministry is nowhere suggested. The theology of one New Testament epistle, Hebrews, specifically precludes the Christian use of this model. In the first century, as the Church was in the process of working out its understanding, theology and structures of ministry, there is no scriptural evidence that the model of levitical priesthood was ever introduced. In the Old Testament the levitical model had developed connotations of power and status, sexism and hierarchy. When it was finally introduced into Christianity, in the second through the fourth centuries, hierarchical status and power and the exclusion of women from official ministry appeared at the same time.

Both priesthood and ordination are post-biblical concepts. Ministry in the New Testament is described in terms of discipleship and service. The disciple is a person who is bound in close, loving, and learning relationship to Jesus. The disciple is called to be like his or her master, to be a servant. The service of the Christian disciple may be understood as priestly through the model of the priesthood of the suffering servant. The priesthood of gratuitous self-offering in atoning love is authentic Christian ministry. The levitical model of priesthood of power and status cannot be authentic Christian ministry.

The early Church experimented with other models of ministry which it found in the Old Testament tradition of the ministry of word. There were Christian teachers and disciples, apostles, prophets and elders. There is evidence in the New Testament of the participation of women in all of these offices, with the sole exception of that of elder which was rooted in patriarchal tradition. The office of elder, however, soon ceased to exist in the Church as it was merged with other offices.

In 1976 the majority of the members of the Pontifical Biblical Commission in Rome voted to affirm that scripture does not give

CONCLUSION

sufficient evidence to exclude the possibility of the ordination of women to ministerial office in the Church today.[1] The Vatican "Declaration on the Question of the Admission of Women to the Ministerial Priesthood," which was issued in the same year, asked whether the Church could depart from the attitude and practice of Jesus and the apostles as reported in scripture and considered normative in the Church.[2] The Declaration itself had an interpretation of the attitude and practice of Jesus and the early Church very different from that of the Pontifical Biblical Commission or that presented in this book. Its interpretation was determined by theology and magisterium, rather than by biblical scholarship. The 1978 "Research Report" of the Catholic Theological Society of America challenged the Vatican Declaration on precisely this point.[3] Its conclusions support the interpretation of the biblical evidence which has been put forth in this book.

The magisterium of the Church has itself called for the equality of women in all areas.[4] The only area in which women are still today excluded from equality in and by the Church itself is the exclusion of women from the Church's call to serve Jesus in the fulness of sacramental ministry. The Church has justified this exclusion on the basis of tradition. Yet the Church has also consistently taught that its tradition and practice must be conformed to the norm of scripture.

The crux of the problem lies in the interpretation of scripture. Scholars today are realizing that the interpretation of scriptural texts about women have long been influenced by the misogynistic biases of male commentators. Since scholars have now become aware of such influences, they are better able to eliminate them from future understanding of scripture. The study of sacred scripture is a developing science, which changes with and builds upon new discoveries. Current biblical scholarship is in the process of rediscovering the prominent role of women in ministry in the New Testament. New understanding in this area, as has happened in other areas of biblical scholarship in the past, will finally come to influence and affect the life of every Christian in the Church.

Long ago, in a letter to the Christians of Galatia, Paul proclaimed that in Christ there is neither Jew nor Greek, slave nor free, male nor female.[5] In spite of this theology of Paul, all three dichotomies have existed within the history of the Church. The first was overcome in the first century, with the aid of Paul himself. The second was not overcome until the nineteenth century. In both cases the process of moral insight and change involved controversy, pain and division. It is time now for the Church to repudiate the third dichotomy and to suffer the pain which that may entail. Pain and division are not inherently evil, but very much a part of biblical tradition. And suffering, as the New Testament affirms, leads to the birth of new life.

NOTES

1. Pontifical Biblical Commission, "Report," *Origins* 6 (1976) pp. 92–96.

2. 1976 Vatican Declaration, 18.

3. Catholic Theological Society of America, "Research Report: Women in Church and Society" (Bronx, N. Y.: Catholic Theological Society of America, 1972), pp. 21–23.

4. Vatican II, *Gaudium et spes,* 29, trans. in Abbott, *op. cit.,* pp. 227–228: "every type of discrimination, whether social or cultural, whether based on sex, race, color, social condition, language, or religion, is to be overcome and eradicated as contrary to God's intent. For in truth it must still be regretted that fundamental personal rights are not yet being universally honored. Such is the case of a woman denied the right and the freedom to choose . . . a state of life, or to acquire an education or cultural benefits equal to those recognized for men."

5. Gal 3:28.

APPENDIX

WOMEN AND PRIESTLY MINISTRY: THE NEW TESTAMENT EVIDENCE

In August 1976 the Executive Board of the Catholic Biblical Association of America appointed a committee of prominent scholars from its membership to study and report on the Role of Women in Early Christianity. This Committee developed into a Task Force whose members are Madeleine Boucher, Richard J. Dillon, John R. Donahue, Elisabeth Schussler Fiorenza, Eugene H. Maly, Sandra M. Schneiders, and Richard J. Sklba. The following statement is a précis of the ongoing discussion of the Task Force. The Executive Board directs it to be published in the Catholic Biblical Quarterly as part of the official record of the 1979 annual meeting and commends it to the membership.

This statement presents a brief examination of the NT evidence concerning the role of women in the Church and a conclusion. It is not an exhaustive study, but addresses biblical arguments commonly advanced in the current Roman Catholic discussion on the question of women and priestly ministry.*

*Arguments for and against the admission of women to priestly ministry are discussed in the following official statements and reports: Catholic Theological Society of America, *A Report on the Status of Women in Church and Society: Considered in Light of the Question of Women's Ordination* (Mahwah, NJ: Darlington Seminary, 1978); National Conference of Catholic Bishops, *Theological Reflections on the Ordination of Women* (Washington: USCC, 1972; also in *JES* 10 [1973] 695–99); Pontifical Biblical Commission, "Can Women Be Priests?," *Origins* 6 (July 1, 1976) 92–96; Sacred Congregation for the Doctrine of the Faith, "Declaration on the Question of the Admission of Women to the Ministerial Priesthood," *Origins* 6 (February 3, 1977) 517–24 (also pub. with Commentary [Washington: USCC, 1977]; compare L. and A. Swidler, eds., *Women Priests: A Catholic Commentary on the Vatican Declaration* [New York: Paulist Press, 1977]).

In adducing NT evidence for use in the theological discussion, the exegete recognizes the nature and the limitations of the sources, and the necessity for careful and critical interpretation. As has long been known, we do not have in the NT an exact or complete record of the ministry of Jesus or the development of the early Church. Material in the Gospels and Acts for example, transmitted orally for some time after the historical events it narrates, was already subjected to the process of selection and theological interpretation before and during its literary composition. In other books, such as the epistles, we have fragments of information about the early Church which surfaced perhaps because the author dealt with a particular problem in a local church, as when Paul wrote to Corinth, or incidentally, as in greetings to members of a community. The NT provides no discussion of the role of women in the ministry of Jesus or the early Church, but only occasional and limited information. Following is an historical-critical assessment of that evidence in light of the current discussion.

Ministry and Ministries in the Early Church

The Christian priesthood as we know it began to be established no earlier than the end of the first or beginning of the second century. In the primitive Church before this, ministries were complex and in flux, and the different services later incorporated into the priestly ministry were performed by various members of the community. As the list of charisms in Eph 4:11 shows, ministry was diversified: "And his gifts were that some should be apostles, some prophets, some evangelists, some pastors and teachers." (Cf. Paul's list in 1 Cor 12:28: apostles, prophets, teachers, miracle workers, healers, helpers, administrators, speakers in tongues; and 1 Cor 12:4–11; Rom 12:4–8.) Paul speaks of ministries as "gifts that differ according to the grace given to us" (Rom 12:6); and he says of them that the Spirit "apportions to each one individually as he wills" (1 Cor 12:11). The diverse charisms have but one source: God, through the Spirit, bestows them as he chooses (1 Cor 12:4–11, 18, 28). They also have a single purpose: just as the members of a body have different functions which work together for the good of the whole, so the different charisms are given to individuals for the common good, "for the work of ministry, for building up the body of Christ" (Eph 4:12; cf. vv 15–16; 1 Cor 12:7, 12–31; Rom 12:4–5). Thus, while Paul could speak of charisms as varying in importance with respect to "upbuilding," the NT evidence does not indicate that one group controlled or exercised all ministries in the earliest Church. Rather the responsibility for ministry, or service, was shared by various groups within the community.

Women in the NT

Central in the NT is the conviction that the kingdom of God has broken into history and that the old social order is transformed: now, by virtue of baptism in Christ, "there is neither Jew nor Greek, there is neither slave nor free, there is no 'male and female'" (Gal 3:28, with reference to Gen 1:27). That this conviction was implemented with respect to women both in Jesus' ministry and in the early Church, to the extent allowed by cultural possibilities, can scarcely be doubted. Women were among the disciples, or followers, of Jesus from the beginning and they were faithful to the end (Mark 15:40 – 41, 47; 16:1; Luke 8:1–3). The women, most prominent of whom was Mary Magdalene, were the first to discover the empty tomb (Mark 16:2–8; Luke 24:1–11) and, according to some Gospel traditions, the first to see the Risen Lord (Matt 28:1–10; John 20:11–18); and they were among those designated by him as his witnesses (Luke 24:48; cf. 24:22, 33). In Paul's view, the requisites for apostleship were to have seen the Risen Lord and received a commission to proclaim the gospel (1 Cor 9:1–2; 15:8–11; Gal 1:11–17), and in Luke's view, to have accompanied Jesus during his ministry as well. Women thus actually met the criteria for apostleship. Women were admitted to baptism and membership in the Church, without qualification, from the outset (unlike the Gentiles). Women were members of the earliest community which formed the nucleus of the Church (Acts 1:14 – 15) and were among those who received the Spirit at Pentecost (Acts 2:1– 4). Ministry, which derives from the gifts of the Spirit communicated by baptism, was open to women.

There is evidence that many of the functions which later were associated with the priestly ministry were in fact exercised by women, and no evidence that women were excluded from any of them. There were women instrumental in the founding of churches (Acts 18:2, 18–19 with 1 Cor 16:19 and Rom 16:3–5); women in leadership roles (Rom 16:1–2, 6, 12; Phil 4:2–3); women with functions in public worship (1 Cor 11:5); women engaged in teaching converts (Acts 18:26). Women prophets are attested (1 Cor 11:5; Acts 21:9). In Paul's greetings at the conclusion of Romans, a woman minister (*diakonos*) of the church at Cenchreae is named (Phoebe: Rom 16:1, cf. 1 Tim 3:8, 11), and very likely a woman apostle (Junia: Rom 16:7). Thus, while male leaders may have been more prominent and numerous in the early Church, and while women's activities may have been somewhat limited by what was culturally permissible, many roles which ultimately were associated with the priestly ministry were evidently never restricted to men.

The limitations presently placed on women's role in the Church and the arguments advanced in support of those restrictions must be evaluated in light of the evidence for ministerial co-responsibility and for the presence of women in ministries in the Church of the NT period.

The Praxis of Jesus and the Apostles

The assertion that the attitude of Jesus and the apostles provides a permanent norm excluding women from ordained priestly ministry in the Church presents difficulties of both a theoretical and an historical kind.

The most serious logical difficulty lies in the claim that the source for such a norm is the intention of Jesus. Only a conscious theological decision could provide a clear imperative; but it cannot be shown that a theological decision was made to exclude women from priestly ministry. All that is known is that there were no women, Gentiles, Samaritans, or, evidently, slaves among the Twelve; it is not possible to deduce from that fact a conscious intention rather than unconscious social and cultural motivation. That becomes clear when we pose the question whether in choosing the Twelve Jesus intended to establish criterion for office in respect to sex, but not in respect to race, ethnic identity, or social status.

The argument raises, in addition, many exegetical and historical difficulties by failing to take into account the complexity and unclarity of the origins of the Christian priestly ministry as we know it. The circle of Twelve is the only exclusively male group associated with Jesus; but the Twelve, while usually regarded as predecessors of the later Church officials called priests, are not their sole precursors. Jesus did not ordain the Twelve; according to the Gospels he appointed them, on the model of the patriarchs, to "sit on twelve thrones, judging the twelve tribes of Israel" in the new age (Matt 19:28; cf. Luke 22:30). To this eschatological role, the only one belonging exclusively to the Twelve exercised, during Jesus' ministry and in leadership positions of the earliest Church, they were always part of a wider circle not restricted to males. In Jesus' ministry, the Twelve were among the followers, or disciples, of Jesus who included both women and men (Mark 15:40–41; Luke 8:1–3) and who, after the resurrection, formed the nucleus of the primitive Church and provided its leadership

In the earliest Church, the roles and functions which later came to be associated with the priestly ministry were never limited to the Twelve; and some (e.g., administrator of a local church, leader of public worship) are nowhere in the NT explicitly attributed to the Twelve. Neither were they conferred by the Twelve (at least not in every case), but were gifts from God through the Spirit (1 Cor 12:4–11,28). While the Twelve were probably apostles (*apostoloi,* a post-resurrection designation), the circle of apostles was wider, including among others James, Paul and Barnabas. Apostleship (according to the Pauline or Lukan understanding) could neither be conferred nor handed on by succession; Paul expressly disclaims having been made an apostle by men (Gal 1:1). The Christian terminology of priesthood arose in relation to the eucharist, as that gradually came to be understood as sacrifice (e.g., *Did* 14). Very little is known as to who presided at the eucharist in the earlier Church. While it is reasonable to suppose that the Twelve and the missionary apostles were among those who did, our only evidence is that prophets and teachers played this role (*Did.* 10:7, cf. 13:3; Acts 13:1-2); and prophecy, the charism second in importance only to apostleship (1 Cor 12:28; cf. 14:1-5), is one which we are certain was given to women (1 Cor 11:5; Acts 21:9). Other ministries, apparently more significant in the earliest period, such as missionary preaching, teaching of new converts, administration and service of local churches, were exercised by persons who were not members of the Twelve and in many cases not appointed by the Twelve, and who evidently were not exclusively male.

Thus, the claim that the intention and example of Jesus and the example of the apostles provide a norm excluding women from priestly ministry cannot be sustained on either logical or historical grounds.

Disciplinary Regulations

In the NT, it is important to observe, there are no texts which address the specific question of women and Church office. Only three epistolary passages have to do with women in the assembly, and these are no more than disciplinary regulations pertaining to proper conduct. The exclusion of women from Church office can hardly be deduced from these texts. In 1 Cor 11:3-6, Paul instructs women to wear a headdress, that is, to appear in the proper and customary attire, when praying or prophesying, so that these new converts may not appear eccentric. Notwithstanding Paul's attempt to ground it in the order of creation, the Church has acknowledged the cultural contingency of the regulation by no longer imposing it. In 1 Cor 14:33a-35, women are forbidden to speak in the assembly. It must be noted that the verb here is "to speak" (*lalein*) and not "to teach." To interpret the verb "to speak" as meaning "to teach," and to understand these verses as barring women from the official function of teaching, is unwarranted by text and context. The context indicates rather that the prohibition is against asking questions (v 35) or in some way disturbing the assembly (cf. vv 28, 30). It is in a Pastoral epistle, generally assumed to have been written in a later period, that women are admonished not "to teach" (*didaskein*) but to be submissive and silent (1 Tim 2:11-15). That such a prohibition, which could cover speech of all kinds, was not always and everywhere known is certain, since in Paul's mission women not only prayed and prophesied at worship (1 Cor 11:5) but also exercised the ministry of teaching (Acts 18:26). Thus these

three passages, which do limit women's activities to what is decent and accepted, are pastoral directives concerning worship, and they are motivated
by social and cultural factors. They can scarcely be taken as permanent theological norms relating to Church ministry.

The Created Order

Nowhere do the passages cited in the preceeding paragraph invoke
faithfulness to the attitude of Jesus. Rather the authors, alluding to the two
creation stories in Genesis 1 and Genesis 2–3, attempt to ground the disciplinary regulations in a theory of the subordination of woman in creation.
Although Paul draws back from a consistent subordinationist view (1 Cor
11:11–12), he orders the headdress (1 Cor 11:3–16) because the "head"
(source of being) of a woman is her husband (v 3) and because man is the image and reflected glory of God, while woman is the reflected glory of man (v
7), since woman was made from and for man (vv 8–9, and cf. the similar argument in 1 Tim 2:13–15). But if these disciplinary injunctions are culturally and historically limited, so, much more importantly, is the theological
anthropology on which they are based. The presuppositions of Paul's patriarchal culture have influenced his interpretation of Genesis. Certainly an anthropology in which woman is subordinate to man cannot be derived from
the first creation account which—unlike Paul—speaks of the two sexes of
humanity, created at the same time, as equally in God's image: "in the image
of God he created him ['ādām, humanity]; male and female he created
them" (Gen 1:27; cf. Gen 5:1–2). Neither can it be derived from the second
creation account, where it is the likeness and unity of the pair, made from
one human being ('ādām), that is stressed (bones of bones, flesh of flesh,
woman ['iššā] from man ['iš]; Gen 2:23. According to both accounts, man
and woman are equal in the created order. It is only later in the second account that, in an etiology, woman's subordination in the social order is ascribed to sin (Gen 3:17); it is a consequence of the dis-ordering of the created
order. Paul is truer to the Genesis accounts when, in Gal 3:28; he speaks of a
restoration in Christ of the original equality of creation (cf. Col 3:10–11).

Conclusion

An examination of the biblical evidence shows the following: that there
is positive evidence in the NT that ministries were shared by various groups
and that women did in fact exercise roles and functions later associated with
priestly ministry; that the arguments against the admission of women to
priestly ministry based on the praxis of Jesus and the apostles, disciplinary
regulations, and the created order cannot be sustained. The conclusion we
draw, then, is that the NT evidence, while not decisive by itself, points toward the admission of women to priestly ministry.

SELECT BIBLIOGRAPHY

Chapter One: Women in Greece, Rome and Judaism

Aristotle, *Politics.*

Arthur, Marylin B. "Classics." *Signs* 2(1976) 382–403.

Balsdon, J.P.V.D. *Roman Women.* London: Bodley Head, 1962.

Gomme, Arthur. "The Position of Women in Athens in the Fifth and Fourth Centuries B.C." *Classical Philology* 20(1925) 1–25. Reprinted in A. Gomme. *Essays in Greek History and Literature.* Oxford: Blackwell, 1937.

Josephus. *Against Apion. Antiquities. Jewish War.*

Kitto, H.D.F. *The Greeks.* Baltimore: Penguin, 1951.

Lefkowitz, Mary and Fant, Maureen. *Women in Greece and Rome.* Toronto: Samuel-Stevens, 1977.

Malherbe, Abraham (Ed.). *The Cynic Epistles.* Missoula, MT.: Scholars Press, 1977.

Oepke, A. *"Gyne." TDNT* I, 776–789.

Peritz, Ismar J. "Women in the Ancient Hebrew Cult." *Journal of Biblical Literature* 17(1898) 111–148.

Philo. *De Opificio Mundi. De Specialibus Legibus. In Flaccum. Hypothetica. Legum Allegoriarum.*

Plato. *Republic. Laws.*

Plutarch. *Lives. Moralia.*

Pomeroy, Sarah B. *Goddesses, Whores, Wives and Slaves.* New York: Schocken, 1975.

Seltmann, Charles. *Women in Antiquity.* London: Thames & Hudson, 1956.

Swidler, Leonard. *Women in Judaism.* Metuchen, N.J.: Scarecrow, 1976.

Vos, Clarence. *Women in Old Testament Worship.* Delft: Judels & Brinkman, 1968.

Chapter Two: Biblical Foundations of Ministry
A. Old Testament

Abba, R. "Priests and Levites." *IDB* III, 876–889.

150 BIBLIOGRAPHY

Baudissin, Wolf von. "Priests and Levites." Hastings, J.(Ed). *Dictionary of the Bible* IV, 67–97. Edinburgh: Clark, 1902.

Berry, G. R. "Priests and Levites." *Journal of Biblical Literature* 42(1923) 227–238.

Burkill, T. A. "Sanhedrin." *IDB* IV, 214–218.

Castelot, John J. "Religious Institutions of Israel." *JBC* II, 703–735.

Cody, Aelred. *A History of Old Testament Priesthood. Analecta Biblica* 35. Rome: Pontifical Biblical Institute, 1969.

De Vaux, Roland. *Ancient Israel.* 2 Volumes. New York: McGraw-Hill, 1961.

Eichrodt, Walther. *Theology of the Old Testament.* Volume I. Philadelphia: Westminister, 1961.

Emerton, J. A. "Priests and Levites in Deuteronomy." *Vetus Testamentum* 1 (1962) 129–138.

Gray, George Buchanan. *Sacrifice in the Old Testament.* Oxford: Clarendon, 1925.

Hanson, Paul D. *The Dawn of Apocalyptic.* Philadelphia: Fortress, 1975.

Hoenig, Sidney B. *The Great Sanhedrin.* New York: Bloch, 1953.

Hoonacker Albin van. *Le sacerdoce lévitique dans la loi et dans l'histoire des Hébreux.* London: Williams & Norgate, 1899.

Johnson, A. R. *The Cultic Prophet in Ancient Israel.* Cardiff: University of Wales Press, 1962.

Judge, H.G. "Aaron, Zadok and Abiathar." *Journal of Theological Studies* n.s. 7(1956) 70–74.

Kennett, R. H. "The Origin of the Aaronite Priesthood." *JTS* 6(1905) 161–186.

Krauss, Hans-Joachim. *Worship in Israel.* Richmond: Knox, 1966.

Levy, Isaac. *The Synagogue: Its History and Function.* London: Vallentine-Mitchell, 1963.

Lindhagen, Curt. *The Servant Motif in the Old Testament.* Uppsala: Lundequist, 1950.

Lohse, E. *"Synhedrion." TDNT* VII 860–871.

Martin, Jochen. *Der Priesterliche Dienst.* III. *Quaestiones Disputatae* 48. Herder: Freiburg, 1972.

Meek, T.J. "Aaron and the Sadocites." *American Journal of Semitic Languages* 45(1929) 149–166.

Mohler, James A. *The Origin and Evolution of the Priesthood.* New York: Alba, 1970.

Moore, George Foot. *Judaism in the First Centuries of the Christian Era.* 3 Volumes. Cambridge, MS.: Harvard University Press, 1927.

Morgenstern, Julian. "A Chapter in the History of the High Priesthood." *AJSL* 55(1938) 1–24, 183–197, 360–377.

Pedersen, Johannes. *Israel. Its Life and Culture.* Volumes III–IV. London: Oxford University Press, 1940.

Priesterbild im Wandel. Festschrift zum 70. Geburtstag A. Gruber. Linz: Landesverlag, 1972.

Rowley, H. H. "Early Levite History and the Question of the Exodus." *Journal of Near Eastern Studies* 3(1944) 73–78.

"Melchizedek and Zadok (Gn 14 and Ps 110)." *Festschrift Alfred Bertholet zum 80. Geburtstag.* Tübingen: Mohr. 1950, p. 461–472.

The Rediscovery of the Old Testament. London: Clarke, 1946.

Worship in Ancient Israel. London: S.P.C.K., 1967.

"Zadok and Nehustan." *Journal of Biblical Literature* 58(1939) 113–141.

Sabourin, Leopold. *Priesthood.* Leiden: Brill, 1973.

Schrage, W. *"Synagoge."* *TDNT* VII, 798–852.

Sonne, I. "Synagogue." *IDB* IV, 476–491.

Wright, G. E. "The Levites in Deuteronomy." *Vetus Testamentum* 4(1954) 325–333.

B. New Testament

Audet, Jean-Paul. *Structures of Christian Priesthood.* New York: Macmillan, 1967.

Beyer, H. W. *"Diakoneo."* *TDNT* II, 81–93.

Bornkamm, G. *"Presbys, presbyteros."* *TDNT* VI, 651–683.

Cohauz, Otto. *The Priest and St. Paul.* New York: Benziger, 1927.

Colson, Jean. *Ministère de Jésus-Christ ou le sacerdoce de l'Évangile.* Paris: Beauchesne, 1966.

Concilium. Volumes 34, 71, 74, 80.

Congar, Yves. *Priest and Layman.* London: Dorton, Longman & Todd, 1967.

Cullmann, Oscar. *The Christology of the New Testament.* Philadelphia: Westminster, 1959.

Delorme, Jean. "Diversité et unité des ministères d'après le Nouveau Testament." *Le ministère et les ministères selon le Nouveau Testament.* Paris: Seuil, 1973, pp. 283–346.

Dix, Gregory. "The Ministry in the Early Church." Kirk, Kenneth E. *The Apostolic Ministry.* London: Hodder & Stoughton, 1946, pp. 183–303.

Dunn, James D. *Jesus and the Spirit.* Philadelphia: Westminster, 1975.

Farrar, A. M. "The Ministry in the New Testament." Kirk, *Apostolic Ministry,* 113–182.

Feuillet, André. *The Priesthood of Christ and His Ministers.* Garden City, N.Y.: Doubleday, 1975.

Fuller, Reginald H. *The Foundations of New Testament Christology.* New York: Scribner's, 1965.

Jeremias, Joachim. *Jerusalem in the Time of Jesus.* Philadelphia: Fortress, 1969.

———. *"Pais theou." TDNT* V, 654–717.

———. *The Prayers of Jesus. Studies in Biblical Theology.* 2nd Series, Vol. 6. Naperville, Ill.: Allenson, 1967.

Lemaire, André. *Les ministères aux origines de l'Église. Lectio Divina* 68. Paris: Cerf, 1971.

Maly, Eugene H. (Ed.). *The Priest and Sacred Scripture.* Washington: U.S.C.C., 1972.

Manson, T. W. *Ministry and Priesthood.* Richmond: Knox, 1958.

Martin, Jochen. *Die Genese des Amtspriestertums in der frühen Kirche. Quaestiones Disputatae* 48. Freiburg: Herder, 1972.

McKenzie, John L. *Authority in the Church.* New York: Sheed & Ward, 1966.

Ministères et laïcat. Taizé: Presses de Taizé, 1964.

Pesch, Wilhelm. "Priestertum und Neues Testament." *Priestertum—Kirchliches Amt zwischen Gestern und Morgen.* Aschaffenburg: Pattloch, 1971, pp. 10–35.

Priesthood and Prophecy in Christianity and Other Religions. Rome: Gregorian University Press, 1973.

Rahner, Karl. *The Priesthood.* New York: Herder 1973.

Rengstorf, K.H. *"Apostolos." TDNT* I, 407–447.

———. *"Dodeka." TDNT* II, 321–328.

———. *"Mathetes." TDNT* IV, 415–461.

Schelke, Karl Hermann. *Discipleship and Priesthood.* New York: Herder 1965. *Studies in Biblical Theology* 32. London: S.C.M., 1961.

Schweizer, Eduard. *Church Order in the New Testament. Studies in Biblical Theology* 32. London: SCM, 1961.

Shepherd, Massey. "Elder in the New Testament." *IDB* II, 73–75.

Smith, Jerome. *A Priest Forever. A Study of Typology and Eschatology in Hebrews.* London: Sheed & Ward, 1969.

von Campenhausen, Hans. *Kirchliches Amt und geistliche Vollmacht in den ersten drei Jahrhunderten.* Tübingen: Mohr. 1953.

Chapter Three: Ministries of Women in the New Testament

Brown, Raymond E. "Roles of Women in the Fourth Gospel." *Theological Studies* 36(1975) 688–699.

Brown, Raymond E., Donfried, Karl P., Fitzmyer, Joseph A., and Reumann, John (Eds.). *Mary in the New Testament.* Philadelphia/New York: Fortress/Paulist, 1978.

Butler, Sara (Ed.). *Research Report: Women in Church and Society.* Catholic Theological Society of America, 1978.

Daniélou, Jean. *The Ministry of Women in the Early Church.* London: Faith Press, 1961.

Fiorenza, Elisabeth Schüssler. "Feminist Theology as a Critical Theology of Liberation." *Theological Studies* 36(1975) 605–626.
Der Vergessene Partner. Düsseldorf: Patmos, 1964.

Gardiner, Anne Marie (Ed.). *Women and Catholic Priesthood.* New York: Paulist, 1976.   footnote p. 13 6

Gryson, Roger. *The Ministry of Women in the Early Church.* Collegeville, MN.: Liturgical Press, 1976.

Parvey, Constance F. "The Theology and Leadership of Women in the New Testament." Ruether, R. R. (Ed.). *Religion and Sexism.* New York: Simon & Schuster, 1974, pp. 117–149.

Stuhlmueller, Carroll (ed.). *Women and Priesthood.* Collegeville, Mn.: Liturgical Press, 1978.

Swidler, Leonard and Swidler, Arlene (Eds.). *Women Priests.* New York: Paulist, 1977.

Tavard, George H. *Women in Christian Tradition.* Notre Dame, Ind.: University of Notre Dame, 1972.

Trible, Phyllis. "Depatriarchalizing Biblical Interpretation." *Journal of the American Academy of Religion* 41(1973) 30–47.

van der Meer, Haye. *Women Priests in the Catholic Church?* Philadelphia: Temple University, 1973.

footnote 101 Junia

+ Fiorenza p. 88

INDEX OF BIBLICAL REFERENCES

INDEX OF AUTHORS

INDEX OF BIBLICAL WOMEN